An integral Book of the Dead

to Kerstin Kempe

Thank you for 30 years of friendship - I´ll catch up with you later

Wulf Mirko Weinreich

An integral Book of the Dead

meditation and guidance to the terminal care

Translated by Anke Bosse

With an essay by Ken Wilber

ISBN: 978-3-7519-3125-0

Weinreich, Wulf Mirko (2020)
An integral Book of the Dead
    – meditation and guidance to the terminal care
    With an essay by Ken Wilber
Printed & published: BoD – Books on Demand GmbH, Norderstedt (Germany)

German original edition 2009:
    Das andere Totenbuch (ISBN: 978-3-8391-0645-7)
    Printed & published: BoD, Norderstedt (Germany)
© 2009 & 2020 by Wulf Mirko Weinreich, Leipzig (Germany)
© Essay: Ken Wilber 2020
    All rights reserved
English translation: Anke Bosse
Correction: Cindy Lorenz, Illona and Michael Fuchs
Illustrations & layout: Wulf Mirko Weinreich

Contents

Every human being is an attempt of the pure consciousness to become conscious of itself …

Introduction

The purpose of this book is to enable people in a simple way to be good supporters for those who are dying. Nowadays we tend to delegate everything to "specialists", even dying. But there are times when specialists are not available or the person dying is so close to us that we do not want anyone else to get involved. And in the end, we all have to die some day—so taking care of others may be a good preparation. For this reason, this book has been set up in such a way that it can also be used as a meditation help.

The issue of death has played an important role in my life ever since my youth. While in high school I had a summer job at a local undertakers—a coincidence I did not learn to appreciate until years later. After that I was very often faced with the issue of suicide. Also, I—like everybody else—experienced the death of family members. My grandmother's death impressed me the most. She crossed that threshold very consciously. In addition, working a few months in a palliative care unit made the subject accessible to me from even yet another point of view. Finally, some extraordinary states of consciousness of my own—especially some near death experiences—gave me insights into realms beyond those of our regular day-to-day awareness. My involvement with Ken Wilber's philosophy and the Eastern approach to death taught me that some of the realms of consciousness one can experience in meditation very closely resemble different states of death.

By now, there are good books to accompany the dying and their supporters in preparing for death or to help the surviving family members deal with that event[1]. The books of Elisabeth Kübler-Ross, Raymond Moody and others have acquainted us with the phenomenon of near death experiences. But what comes after that last breath? In my own experience, the "Tibetan Book of the Dead", the "Bardo Thodol", offers the best systematization of all that follows after death[2]. Its text, however, uses a language full of metaphors and symbols that one can virtually only understand after having studied Tibetan Buddhism. And finally, when I was once again faced with the issue of death and desperate that there were no texts available in a comprehensible language for the "beyond", I decided to write that book myself. My major concern was to translate the essential stages of the "Bardo Thodol" into a contemporary language and mindset with the help of my psychological, theological, and philosophical knowledge. It was, however, not my objective to create a new scientific interpretation but to compile a practical guide for simple use. Although based upon Ken Wilber's Integral Philosophy[3], I have tried to approach this subject to make it easy for all to understand.

This book begins with an extended introduction by clarifying what happens during death from a mental as well as spiritual point of view. It then provides suggestions showing how to practically support a dying person. Later on, descriptive texts alternate with passages that may be read to the dying person[4] to give them some guidance as to what will follow after death. In Tibet, the dying person is read to from the "Bardo Thodol" for 49 days following death. ("Bardo Thodol" literally means "concerning liberation by hearing in the interim state"). I believe that this custom can easily be applied in the West with appropriate texts.

The finer grasp of this book is based on the presupposition that you, the reader, is working under the assumption that consciousness may not just be a phenomenon subordinate to matter, but rather one that exists parallel to matter, or indeed the very phenomenon upon which matter is based. To me, consciousness is not synonymous with thoughts, memories, pictures, or feelings—these are forms of consciousness just as one can call people, animals, plants or rocks forms of matter. The term "pure CONSCIOUSNESS" used in this book is Wilber's "consciousness per se" or "unity" and is similar to Hegel's "GEIST", Buddhism's "Dharmakāya" or Hinduism's "Brahman" or "the Divine" beyond all religions. Since "pure CONSCIOUSNESS" has no attributes, it eludes description and thus forms a paradox which is fully illustrated in the following poem:

... the one appearing as two
nothing appearing as everything
the absolute appearing as the particular
emptiness appearing as fullness
the uncaused appearing as the caused
oneness appearing as separation
subject appearing as object
the singular appearing as plurality
the impersonal appearing as the personal
the unknown appearing as the known.

It is silence sounding and stillness moving
and these words appearing as pointers
to the wordless
 ... and yet nothing is happening.[5]

The term "emptiness" that contains "all that exists" as evanescent form while simultaneously permeating it may be seen as an analogy for pure CONSCIOUSNESS. This is, however, just another metaphor, an image, the unsatisfactory stammering of an attempt to describe the unnamable. The idea alone that it could be a three-dimensional space without matter like a vacuum is misleading, as even this space is within that "emptiness". And even time is nothing but a finite form within the "emptiness". The mind cannot grasp the paradoxical nature of pure CONSCIOUSNESS. All mystical religions therefore paraphrase this entity that exceeds all our human comprehensive faculties while being the basis of all existence with words that point towards the unnamable such as "Yahweh" (the unspeakable name), "Wakan Tanka" (the great mystery) or "Tao" (the ineffable). The commandment in Christian and Islamic religions "You shall not make for yourself a carved image" refers to that as well. It is sometimes possible, however, to directly experience this entity. This experience is absolutely existential and people frequently describe it as a bright, clear light.

Science approaches this phenomenon from a different point of view: Quantum physics discusses the possibility that our four-dimensional universe may actually be embedded within a higher-dimensional reality. Since our usual waking consciousness is shaped by four-dimensional space-time, this signifies that we simply cannot perceive any dimensions extending beyond. Here again, reality eludes the comprehensive capacities of mankind. Furthermore, these scientists increasingly acknowledge the particular role that information plays in our universe. I am, however, cautious to use their theories to explain psychic processes so as not to believe something to be identical that possibly is just analogous, or to see causal connections where there are only correlations.

Unfortunately the *art of dying*, the "Ars moriendi", has been all but lost in our culture. Few people nowadays prepare for death. Most of us repress it and for those who actually think of it, many probably hope that it will come suddenly and be done with quickly, preferably so quickly that they won't even notice anything. And yet, death might well be life's culmination. From birth on, we invariably move towards this event that I like to call "excarnation" to emphasize that it is nothing other than birth in reverse.

Dying is a period of time that reveals where one is in his growth. At the same time, this phase represents an opportunity to progress further. This is not only true for the conscious completion of one's own life but also for the realization of the true nature of one's own awareness while dying. Supporting this realization is the main purpose of the "Bardo Thodol". It starts from the premise that one constantly moves in intermediate or transitional phases which are called "Bardos". The only unchanging, infinite and eternal is the empty awareness and can be perceived as extreme brightness during dying which is why I call it the "clear light of pure CONSCIOUSNESS" in this book. The transference into the integral context presents a minor linguistic problem: While Wilber's "states of consciousness" (manifest/gross, subtle/fine, causal/empty and nondual) are mostly identical with the intermediate phases of the "Bardo Thodol", they nevertheless need to be distinguished since the Tibetan Bardos comprise a time component, i.e. their duration is noted. In the explanatory passages, the meaning emerges from the context. I have refrained from using Wilber's terms in the texts that are read to the person dying. In those passages, "state" therefore always refers to the "intermediate state" (Bardo).

The "Tibetan Book of the Dead" speaks of a total of six Bardos of which three refer to dying:

1. The moment of death (from the moment of death to the 3rd or 4th day thereafter)
2. The experience of the subtle reality (up to the 14th day)
3. Preparation for a new birth (up to the 49th day).

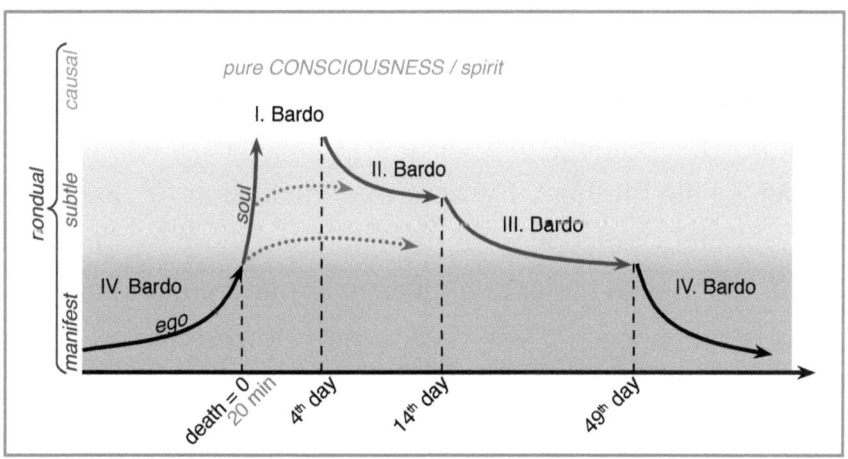

These specific indications of time should be used carefully, however, since our linear time is bound to the material world. In the subtle or causal states of consciousness, on the other hand, time is experienced as "now" or "absent" ("before time").

There are 3 more Bardos that refer to life:
4. Normal daytime consciousness
5. Sleep
6. Meditation

From an integral point of view, the 1st Bardo refers to the causal or nondual state of consciousness / deep sleep, the 2nd Bardo to a very subtle state as experienced in deep dream sleep while the 3rd Bardo refers to a subtle state / light dream sleep (Wilber calls this state "astral" or "psychic"). Although we know of these states, we are not usually aware of them. The 4th Bardo corresponds with our normal, daytime consciousness. Sogyal Rinpoche places emphasis on the differences in the intensity of the sleep phases (5th Bardo) as opposed to the phases of death—it is not for nothing that sleep is sometimes referred to as "death's little brother". He describes meditation (6th Bardo) as the conscious perception of daytime consciousness—in other words that which I refer to elsewhere as the "here and now" or "ego transcendence". Very deep forms of meditation like the Yangtik method described in the following may also lead to subtle, causal, and nondual states of consciousness. You could thus say that sleep is an unconscious trip to the subtler states while dwelling in the 4th Bardo, whereas meditation allows you to experience those very same states.

For the sake of completion, I should add that the transition from the manifest to the nondual states are flowing transitions and defined by increasing subtlety, non-concreteness and ego-lessness: from the world of concrete, material bodies to the emptiness of pure CONSCIOUSNESS and the nondual understanding that matter and CONSCIOUSNESS have never been separated. Many spiritual schools divide the path from the gross to the nondual states into considerably more than three steps—most often into seven. We find these also in the "Tibetan Book of the Dead", as the Bardos themselves are divided into phases. The path described here—directly from the apparent world into causal emptiness of the death and from there back into a new apparent life via subtle states - is the reverse direction as it is normally experienced in spiritual practice. Step by step, by meditating you find more subtle states up to causal states.

At this point let me add something basic to the issue of dying from the Buddhist perspective: Since life on earth is inescapably characterized by suffering, Buddhists pursue "enlightenment"—or hope to see through the play of relative forms (Samsara)—in life, but no later than in the moment of death. This existential realization, also known as "awakening" or "liberation", suspends the cycle of death and rebirth. The individual consciousness overcomes its separation and dissolves into emptiness and impersonal total consciousness: The drop falls back into the ocean. Due to the dissolution of any individual structure, the line of the soul that can best be thought of as an "awareness field", ceases to exist. The illustration above shows the line of the soul dissolving before entering the emptiness of pure CONSCIOUS-NESS (white). The original nature of ego and soul is just as empty and featureless as the pure "CONSCIOUSNESS per se", they are indeed identical. Each form arising from this—be it gross-material or psychic-subtle—is nothing but a fading manifestation of this pure CONSCIOUSNESS. A transmigration of the soul as such—a stable identity beyond death—is rather regarded as an occupational accident in Tibet revealing the inability of the dying person to at least reach the proximity of the causal state. It suggests lacking consciousness or unresolved karma. The illustration above shows such an incident by the two dotted arrows. Tibetan Buddhism allows only one exception—its institution of "Tulkus"—people who have realized their true nature as pure CONSCIOUSNESS but who deliberately keep going from life to life out of empathy in order to help liberate other living beings as "Bodhisattvas". The Dalai Lama is the best known of said Tulkus.

Buddhist terminal care sees its paramount task in helping the dying person to dissolve all identification—the identification with the body first, followed by that with the I or ego and finally that with the soul. Only then will the dying person realize that he or she is in essence causal CONSCIOUSNESS and that matter, thoughts, feelings and events are but fading manifestations (Samsara) that are created in pure CONSCIOUSNESS itself. This realization may help in attaining final liberation. Even though the dying person is prepared for rebirth in the last phase, this is done reluctantly since everybody hopes for the deceased to eternally enter the causal state. The only exceptions are the above mentioned Tulkus.

Here I beg to differ: Buddhism emerged in a time when the evolution of the external world proceeded so slowly that it was hardly even perceptible and thus life was seen as the eternal re-occurrence of the same forever. Therefore, there was no point re-incarnating other than for empathy. In the meantime, evolution has accelerated and Wilber now postulates a second and equal "evolution towards more abundance" in addition to the "evolution towards more awareness" that has developed through the exploration of the inner world. This means that the relative world of appearances (Samsara) is ever faster differentiating into new, more complex forms while becoming increasingly more aware of itself at the same time. This is what is happening as we humans accumulate more and more knowledge and shape our environment. Even if the whole of the manifest world is but a dream of pure CONSCIOUSNESS, it seems to undergo some kind of directed evolution. In my opinion, this is such an exciting process that it could even be reason enough to voluntarily re-incarnate. May be, it´s more precise to say that there was and is nobody to incarnate - never! Only the pure CONSCIOUSNESS exist, enbodying in human beings again and again. It may even be possible that this kind of reincarnation is an important mechanism in this game of evolution to accumulate knowledge and experiences. I, therefore, do not view the preparation of a dying person for a new life as his not having been mature enough to permanently enter the causal state, but as an offer to voluntarily partake further in this cosmic game. After all, it cannot be wrong to play along as consciously as possible no matter where you are at since, according to Wilber, evolution moves from subconsciousness to selfconsciousness to superconsciousness.

Here now a hint for the doubters among you: It is pretty simple to insist that everything in these pages is nonsense since it cannot be proven. That is not entirely so: Tibetan Buddhism has developed a very simple meditation technique called the Bardo seclusion (Yangtik) to explore the subtle and causal states: The set-up is simple: The person meditating spends 49 days (the duration of the spiritual support after death) alone in a completely dark room. His most important task during this time is to observe himself. This person will most certainly experience most of the described phenomena the dying undergo. The appearance may differ a bit due to cultural differences; the deeper structure, however, will be identical. Thus, meditation fulfills all requirements of a regular scientific experiment, especially when it comes to reproducibility. Western civilization's deeply seated fear of extraordinary states of consciousness led to the use of this procedure as a method of torture (solitary confinement in a dark cell). It owed its efficacy to the fact that people were locked-in, incarcerated against their will in total darkness and that there was nobody to help them integrate the resulting experiences in their regular waking consciousness. These experiences are so extreme that one can easily react with psychotic dissociation which I am mentioning expressly to underline what an extreme challenge the Yangtik meditation presents! In order to keep the introduction at an appropriate length, I have jotted down a number of reflections in the addendum for those of you who would like to know more about the relationship between states of consciousness and Bardos.

Finally, I would like to add a few tips on the practical application of this book: The following chapters each consist of introductory comments and texts printed in *cursive* that are meant to be read out loud to the person dying. I set the first lines in **bold** letters to separate one completed text passage from other passages. In addition, alternatives to texts that regard specific situations are highlighted in gray.

I would also like to encourage you to adapt the texts to your specific situation or to add details that you personally consider important. When you know which religion the dead person was belonging to or which synonym they used for the unnamable entity you could use, if suitable, the words for example "God" or "Allah" etc. instead of "pure CONSCIOUSNESS". What I am describing here, in short, is a universal reality and this knowledge therefore already exists on a deeper level of your own consciousness. If it is true that there is only ONE consciousness, then you cannot do anything wrong. You will only enhance the text with your own unique perspective.

Obviously, when you read this book to a dying person, you are also reading it to yourself. Thus, it not only becomes a form of grief work, but is also a preparation for your own death. And with every renewed reading, you will most probably notice that your understanding of what is happening beyond your mortal life is deepening. It will quiet your own fears of dying, is a good way of saying farewell, and deepens an attitude of love that actually lets the other go.

Should you prefer to use these texts as a guided meditation, I advise you to read the cursive texts without the gray markings. This creates a meditation of approximately 45 minutes. If you would like a slightly more detailed version, you can add the paragraphs identified by a narrow bar which extends the meditation to approximately one hour. Paragraphs identified by a wide bar or shaded in gray should not be used in meditation as they are significant only for the actual spiritual care of the dying. When reading the text to several people at once, you can change the recurring formal address by first name to either "dying" or "traveler". It is advisable to ask those meditating which address they prefer—but "dying" is more powerful. By starting you can use any good trance induction, like a body scan, to prepare the travellers. At the end it´s also useful to have a few phrases to bring the people back to their normal, daytime consciousness.

Preparing To Die

Many people sense it when they enter their final illness and vaguely begin to speak of dying. They may start by using figures of speech such as *"When I'm not here anymore"* or *"It won't be long now."*, etc. Please do not try to stop them. On the contrary, if someone is terminally ill but still pretending that everything will continue the way it always was, try to gently make them understand that life could come to an end, that the outcome of their illness is totally unknown, or even that their condition may not give much cause for hope. Sometimes, fear of death will make a person deny the obvious.

People usually use this time to settle their material affairs. However, since this time is accompanied by very specific psychic phenomena, it also allows the dying to mentally bring life to its conclusion, its completion. During this time the mind often relinquishes some of its control mechanisms which in turn enables parts of the consciousness that have long been suppressed or unconscious to rise to the surface. This includes traumatic experiences in the individual's past as well as transpersonal areas of reality (old age transcendence). This is most apparent with people suffering from Alzheimer's disease. Since our culture does not prepare us for dying, people in this phase are often rather helpless.

You can best support the dying by encouraging them to:

... Sort out their human relationships, i.e. by reopening the lines of communication with specific people or by consciously forgiving themselves or others.

... Consciously (as well as openly) say goodbye to all the important people in their lives.

... Finish or turn over all ongoing projects.

... Review and take stock of their lives.

... Accept newly remembered traumatic experiences as part of their lives. The most important support you can offer in this situation is to create a secure space for their wounded feelings, for example by taking them into your arms and helping them to accept those experiences by acknowledging them with sentences like "Yes, that was bad!".

... Deal with spiritual questions. Since their cognitive filters do not work as perfectly as they once did, they might even perceive things that are concealed from you. So, do not dismiss them prematurely as confused, but try to take them seriously.

You could also sing together or chose a background music that may intensify the opening to "the world thereafter". Music featuring the Tibetan singing bowl (like "Space" by Klaus Wiese) is very effective, as those sounds seem to most resemble the eternal sound one may hear in the subtler states. There are, however, several other musical options that can open the individual consciousness to the transpersonal realms.

The First Intermediate State: Dying

The first phase of dying begins with the rattling breath that sets in a few hours before the moment of physical death and ends approximately 20 minutes after the last breath or beating of the heart. The first Bardo, however, lasts significantly longer—until the 4th day to be precise. During this time the body slowly ceases all biological functions. Psychologically, the gradual withdrawal of the consciousness begins.

It is needless to say that everyone would like to die in a friendly atmosphere. Soft and warm lighting (like candles), flowers, and softened background sounds like silence or the appropriate music (for example the music I recommend in the addendum[6]) may help create the right ambience. You may also sing mantras or hymns to or with the person dying. Lively or emotionally disturbing music like Beethoven or rock music, however, is less appropriate. The music should be adequate to ultimately make everyone feel comfortable.

If possible, lay the dying person on his right side as this facilitates the exit. Tell him that he should remember, if possible, to leave his body through the fontanel at the crown of his head. The Tibetans have a meditation called "Phowa" that specifically practices the exit through the crown during life.

It is of course much more difficult when the dying person is in the hospital: Since death is no longer seen as a part of life, many doctors and the nursing staff get into a flurry of activity at the moment of death—after all, to keep the person alive is their duty. When it becomes apparent that death will occur within the next few hours, ask the physician to attend only to the basic needs (i.e. absence of pain) and to otherwise maintain a low profile— if possible until an hour after the onset of death (it should hardly matter if the inspection of the corpse is delayed a bit). Try to create a calm and relaxed atmosphere during this time. Your mere presence and the fact that you know a little more about dying— even though the situation may prevent you from using that knowledge—will help the dying person find their way.

It is another matter if you are not able to be physically present at the death of a person close to you. In such cases, you can only connect with them mentally and keep calling their name silently. Due to the fact that other rules apply to subtle states, it will hardly reduce their effectiveness if these texts are read even if you are not physically present. You might only be informed of the death of someone close to you after several days have passed. In such cases, it is clearly makes no sense to read texts that are meant to prepare the person for death. Instead, you can start with the text highlighted in gray on page 31.

Even though the end is already in sight, many people unnecessarily prolong their dying because they feel that the people who will survive them keep holding on to them. It may save them much suffering if their relatives explicitly allow them to pass on. You can do that using your own words or with the following text:

"Dear (name of the person dying),
We know your time has come.
Your life on earth is ending.
We shall not stop you.
And we ask you not to show consideration for us.
We shall remember you with love.
We can deal with our grief alone.
Follow your path
To the union with the source of it all,
—The clear light of pure CONSCIOUSNESS—
Or into a new form.
But do not remain here.
Be not afraid of apparitions along the way.
Let them come and go
Without holding on to them or warding them off,
But look upon them with loving serenity.
Do not be afraid that your ego is dissolving
—It will take away your limitations
And give you unknown freedom.
We wish you well on your journey."

You can continue reading the following texts to prepare the person dying for what will happen very soon. Part of it will be the preparation for that overwhelming experience of the extreme brightness that is inherent in the clear light of pure CONSCIOUSNESS. This precious moment can be easily missed in their dazed state. At the actual moment of death, the human body releases a large amount of N,N-DMT and 5-MeO-DMT—two neurotransmitters very closely related to LSD—which seems to be the chemical correlate for the altered states of consciousness that the dying person experiences.[7] At the best, they will pass through some or all of those stages during the process that are described in books that relate to near death experiences. This can include seeing one's own life pass by in fast motion and evaluating it; encountering other beings who are recognized as relatives and friends who have previously passed away, going through a dark tunnel into a clear brilliant light and recognizing this light as the Divine beyond it all and/or experiencing feelings of infinite reassurance, love and coming home, etc. These are, however, only a few of the journey's stages.

In the following, you will find a text that can be read before the actual moment of death to prepare the dying person for the first intermediate state:

"Dear (name of the person dying),
Listen to me and be here in all your attentiveness!
The time of death has arrived for you.
You will soon draw your final breath
And your consciousness will leave your body.
This is an entirely natural process,
Even though it is not always easy.
As you have once entered this world
Through the gateway that is called birth,
You will now leave it through the passage of death.
You have traveled this path uncountable times before,
Even though your conscious mind cannot remember.
But the consciousness beyond the mind knows exactly
How it is done.
Remember that it is better to leave the body
Through the crown of the head.
If you think that it may be of help,
Connect yourself to your true self
Or a protective spiritual being,
Or a spiritual teacher.
Ask them to accompany you on your journey.

Dear (name of the person dying),
Listen to me and be here in all your attentiveness!
Your ego and your identity
Will soon cease to exist
And merge with something vaster.
You will experience realms of reality,
Into which you never entered or rarely had access to
During your physical life.
Out of love and friendship
I want to accompany you on part of this journey.
I shall tell you about 3 intermediate states,
About the 3 stages of the dissolution of the ego.
First you will hear about
The "state of pure CONSCIOUSNESS",
The all-embodying, all-permeating, the all-being
Shining in the most bright and clear light.
Later I shall describe to you
The "state of true being",
The realm of infinite possibilities,
With its fascinating richness of visions and ideas.
And finally you will learn
About the "state of becoming",
Where the subtle prepares
To enter the earthly world.
Do not be afraid of these states,
Because all that you will experience
Are projections of your consciousness.

You will now become aware
Of that which has always been there,
But you were unable to perceive
In the earthly limitation of your mind and senses.
Remember,
You choose the direction you will take
In each of these intermediate states:
The path leading towards dissolution
Into pure CONSCIOUSNESS,
Or the path towards materializing once again
Into a physical body."

In the Tibetan Buddhist practice you alert the dying person directly after the actual moment of death to the fact that they have indeed passed on, that they need not be afraid, and that they should enter the radiant pure CONSCIOUSNESS as soon as possible so that they can thus overcome the limitations and binds of the ego. The following texts for the first Bardo are different in as far as they are repeated several times within the first hour after death to empower that person to quickly and directly enter into pure CONSCIOUSNESS. Later these texts will be read like the other texts just once a day. They are so important that it is advised not to shorten them.

The following text can be repeated several times from shortly before the moment of death until 20 minutes thereafter. It offers an extremely direct opportunity for immediate liberation:

"Dear (name of the person dying),
Listen to me and be here in all your attentiveness!
You are just dying.
Your body is systematically discontinuing its functions,
Its temperature is decreasing more and more.
Your feelings will gradually level out
Until they dissolve entirely,
And your physical mind ceases to work.
Watch yourself now,
You will recognize different stages:
At first it may feel
As though a weight presses down on your body,
Or as though it struggles under an inner strain.
Then you may begin to feel cold,
A cold that turns into warmth,
That turns into heat,
And that culminates in lightness.
That is what is called the "dissolution of the elements".
Relax and allow your center of perception
To sink into your heart.
This is the beginning of the dissolution of your ego.
Everything will now happen at once.
Remain awake and conscious.
Trust that what happens will be right.
Next, you will begin to pull out of your body.
Do that through the crown of your head if you can.
Your consciousness begins to expand.

Your limitations begin to dissolve,
Everything that appeared to be outside before
Is suddenly within you.
You may now perceive
That you are embedded in something infinitively large,
And maybe you can hear a voice calling you from afar.
Follow that voice.
You will very quickly pass through a darkness
That may feel like a tunnel.
After that you will enter into a bright white light:"…

Alternative 1

If hours or even days have passed before you learned of the person's passing, you can begin with the following text:

"Dear (name of the person dying),
Listen to me and be here in all your attentiveness!
Even though the moment of your passing
Happened a few hours (days) ago,
I would like to accompany you in love and friendship
On your transitional journey.
I will tell you about the 3 intermediate states,
About the 3 stages of the dissolution of the ego
So that you may find your path more easily.
Do not fear the apparitions on the path.

31

Receive them lovingly
—They are part of yourself,
Embodied projections of the conscious mind.
Let them come and go
Without holding on or warding them off,
But look upon them with serenity.
You are becoming conscious of what has always been,
But that you, in the material limitation of mind and senses,
Were unable to perceive.
Be not afraid of your ego dissolving
—It will take away your limitations
And give you unknown freedom.
Remember,
In each of these intermediate states
You have the choice of either path:
The path leading towards dissolution
Into pure CONSCIOUSNESS,
As well as the one towards materializing again
Into a physical body.

Dear (name of the person dying),
Hear these words,
You have already left your old body.
And you probably have already
Passed the vast blackness.
Maybe you are just now at
The threshold of a bright white light:"…

Alternative 2

Starting with the second reading you can skip the preparatory texts and start as follows:

"Dear (name of the person dying),
I join with you in love,
In whatever stage of the passage
You may be in just now.

Dear (name of the person dying),
Listen to me and be here in all your attentiveness!
Knowing that you no longer exist
In the way we knew you,
I shall still address you by your old name
Just so my words will be directed to you.
Dear (name of the person dying),
According to terrestrial time,
You died yesterday (2 / 3 / 4 /a few/many days /weeks ago).
You have left your body
And have by now probably passed the vast blackness.
If you have already gone into pure CONSCIOUSNESS,
This repetition will not disturb you.
But should you just be at the threshold
Of a light with unimaginable brightness,
Hear my words: ...

… The clear light is the signal for the first intermediate state,
The "state of pure CONSCIOUSNESS".
This state is beyond all that can be described.
No word could be more than a mere and inadequate inkling,
To illumine the unimaginable, the unnamable.
You could call it empty,
Yet it contains ALL.
You could call it bright and clear,
Yet it is also the cradle of darkness.
When you reach the "state of pure CONSCIOUSNESS"
Remember these words
And you will recognize it as the unimaginable, the unnamable.
Be not afraid of the intensity of its brilliance.
Be not afraid of its vast dimension.
Move towards it.
Enter it and merge with it,
Like a drop of water falling back into the ocean
To dissolve into its endless vastness.
Do not—for love or weakness—
Cling to your body or your old identity,
But overcome the limitations of your small,
Individual consciousness and dissolve entirely
Into the all-embracing pure CONSCIOUSNESS.
Know, that in your true being
You ARE this radiant consciousness,
That you and pure CONSCIOUSNESS
Were never separated.

Know, that what you used to call your "I"
Was nothing but a projection,
A finite apparition
In the infinite ocean of CONSCIOUSNESS.
Know, that your falling out of the unity with
Pure CONSCIOUSNESS was nothing but a trick,
That the identification with the "I" was necessary
To play the cosmic game.
And now that you have figured out the game
You no longer need the separation;
You are able to know yourself as what you truly are:
An egoless self—identical with pure CONSCIOUSNESS.

Dear (name of the person dying),
Perceive the oneness of all living things:
If your true nature is pure CONSCIOUSNESS,
Then pure CONSCIOUSNESS is equally the true nature
Of all other beings—and you were never separated from it.
Understand that you have played hide and seek with yourself:
No matter into whose eyes you looked,
You never saw anyone but yourself:
Pure CONSCIOUSNESS.
Thus this boundless consciousness
Is like a puppet player with a thousand arms,
Playing the show with himself.
Use this realization
To attain love and empathy for all beings.

Dear (name of the person dying),
Understand that the true nature of pure CONSCIOUSNESS
—And thus your own—is:
Ineffable emptiness,
Without content, attribute, beginning and end,
Permeating everything unopposed.
The emptiness of pure CONSCIOUSNESS
Is not the void
But the source and the aim of all phenomena.
Even space and time have come from it
And will in time return there.
Understand that everything, feeling or thought
Are nothing but fleeting forms
In the emptiness of pure CONSCIOUSNESS,
And that none of these phenomena will ever change that.
This emptiness is no state of consciousness
And no level of development.
All states and levels begin and end in it.
Understand that what you called the "earthly realm"
Is but a materialized dream
That is being dreamed in the emptiness
Of pure CONSCIOUSNESS:
Variable forms
That unfold only to disappear again
—Like the clouds that emerge and vanish
Under the clear blue of the empty sky.

Dear (name of the person dying),
Listen to me and be here in all your attentiveness!
Understand that pure CONSCIOUSNESS
Reveals itself in two aspects:
As awareness and as love.
You could also call them witnessing and empathy.
Each phenomenon unfolding in the
Emptiness of pure CONSCIOUSNESS
Is welcomed and accepted
As a unique and always complete creation.
That is what is known as the all-embracing love:
No holding on, no rejection.
Everything, phenomenon, and process may arise,
Borne by and imbued with love,
And may vanish again:
No judgment, no desire for improvement,
Everything is what it is
—This is what love is.

Dear (name of the person dying),
Know now the second aspect of pure CONSCIOUSNESS
In its full consequence:
Awareness, witness, observer.
Do not focus on the forms of consciousness!
Do not concentrate on memories,
Thoughts, feelings or desires

—They are but fleeting phenomena,
Finite, like all other forms.
Look beyond: Who is witnessing all that?
An egoless awareness
—Pure CONSCIOUSNESS—
No thoughts, no feelings,
No desires and no memories,
No content, no form,
No beginning and no end,
Radiant, blissful and silent.

Dear (name of the person dying),
Use now the unclouded clarity of your awareness
To understand the ultimate truth, the highest knowledge:
The one who knows, that which is known,
And knowledge itself are one.
They were never separated.
You ARE the one who realizes,
You ARE the realization,
And you ARE that which is realized:
Pure CONSCIOUSNESS,
Becoming conscious of itself.
If you can embrace this insight
It will liberate you for all time.
You will realize the ultimate awakening,
—Beyond space and time—
And remain there forever in bliss and infinite love."

After about 25 minutes at the earliest the dying person then reaches the next phase of the first intermediate state. While the first phase was characterized by the total absence of any form or force, the second phase brings about the breaking forth of primal energy (Prana) and marks the transition to the second intermediate state:

"Dear (name of the person dying),
Listen to me and be here in all your attentiveness!
Another light may appear to you out of
The infinity of pure CONSCIOUSNESS:
Vital energy.
This primal energy erupts in a great explosion,
Enormous and wild like a volcanic eruption
Glaring like a thousand flashes of lightning.
It comes directly out of the emptiness
Of pure CONSCIOUSNESS.
It is the restlessly burning flame of change,
Which allows for the unfolding of CONSCIOUSNESS
Within a form.
It is the vital force out of which all being is born,
The origin of all creation.
Be not afraid of this force.
Surrender to it.
Merge with it.
Discover its burning, seething and pulsating.
It is part of you as you are part of it.

And remember as well that
The ultimate truth
Resides beyond this enormous stream of energy.
The ultimate truth
Is the brilliant awareness,
The clear light of pure CONSCIOUSNESS,
Emptiness without form or limits,
Loving, all-embracing consciousness
Residing in infinite silence and beyond all change.
That is the ultimate truth.
It is enough to have experienced it.
Keep this knowledge
And you will dwell infinitely in the state of awakening."

Do not touch the dying person's body for one hour after their death to ease their transition to the world beyond. After that they can be washed, dressed and laid out until the fourth day if possible. Remember that it is very important to truly let them go. This can be accomplished much more easily if those people who are present with the deceased have also been informed about the mystery of death. The loss is half as hard when you are aware that death is not just the end but a gateway to a different state of consciousness. There is a big difference between "gone" or "transformed"—even though we may not be able to grasp the transformation in our minds.

The Second Intermediate State

During the dying process, the functions of consciousness that are connected to the brain cease working. Hence, the "I", the manifested mental structure slowly starts to fade away, and with it our identity that results from our life history, the experiences we made, our social roles, our convictions, our self-knowledge and the knowledge of our environment.

A deeper layer of consciousness apart from the waking consciousness, the "subtle shell" continues to exist for a while. It is what Wilber calls the deeper psychic self, or he "soul" (in the literal meaning of the word![8]). From the perspective of the non-dual CONSCIOUSNESS, which made experience through this person, the essence of its individual life remains stored in the subtle areas of the CONSCIOUSNESS.

The soul is formed primarily by two components: Karma and the level of awareness you have reached. Karma (as a pattern of cause and effect) comprises the quintessence of all life experiences as well as probability patterns conditioned by the thinking, feeling and acting in previous lives. In the beginning, the soul still views itself as the individual it was in life since the identification with a name and a personal history are part of this conditioning. The specifics of that last life gradually fade the more the process of dissolution progresses. You could also describe this transition as a change from "brain consciousness" (manifest, 4th Bardo) to "soul" (astral, 3rd Bardo) to "higher soul" ("true self" in the text, very subtle, 2nd Bardo) to pure CON-SCIOUSNESS (entirely impersonal, causal, 1st Bardo).

The "Tibetan Book of the Dead" advises a quick passing through the subtle intermediate states in the hope that the dying person may enter the brilliant pure CONSCIOUSNESS as soon as possible and thus lose any form of identity. The soul is to dissolve entirely into nondual CONSCIOUSNESS "like a drop of water in the ocean" where it then remains eternally, beyond all time. To take all these steps consciously during a lifetime requires a steady spiritual practice in that life and a lot of discipline at the moment of death. This does not of course even apply to all people in Tibet. Many people faint or are very confused when the moment of death arrives. This prevents them from reaching the first Bardo or they do not recognize it. Instead of merging with pure CONSCIOUSNESS they remain as souls in one of the subtle spheres. Yet the Tibetans inherently believe in the possibility to still gain dissolution with pure CON-SCIOUSNESS even if it was not possible to jump directly from the gross into the nondual state. It is therefore helpful to guide them on their path to achieve this. Read from the "Bardo Thodol" to the soul for the following 49 days as it usually remains for some time close to the place of its demise and can hear what is being said and therefore understands its situation. This enables the soul to find its bearings and to take the next steps. And even though phrases like "take steps" and "close to the place of one's demise" are reminiscent of a change of place, this is really about the change of a state of consciousness which includes dimensions beyond our normal understanding of space-time. It is therefore easier for our four-dimensional minds to picture this process as a dissolution of the ego and a simultaneous expansion without any change in place. This is why the picture of a drop falling back into and completely merging with the ocean is pretty accurate. And yet, it is just this dissolution of individuality to an impersonal "CONSCIOUSNESS per se" that touches a basic Western fear: "Who am I, if I am nothing?" The answer: "Everything!" does not really sound that comforting to most of us. This fear of the loss of identity is often the reason that a complete awakening is prevented.

A soul that has not been able to make the direct transition from the gross to the nondual states, but is still bound to the subtle spheres, could thence choose the opposite direction and decide to reincarnate instead of blending into CONSCIOUSNESS. This is a problem for the Tibetan mind: The incomplete dissolution of the ego with its probability patterns stored in the soul will shape the thoughts, feelings, and actions in the new life (Karma)—and even more so the case should very little have been dissolved. But this could also be interpreted positively from the integral point of view: Abilities acquired in a past life are woven into the fabric of the new life as talents; you don't have to start from scratch in that new life; evolution is accelerated.

The second Bardo, also called the "intermediate state of true being", is the realm of unlimited possibilities that strive to unfold: CONSCIOUSNESS wants to recognize itself. It closely corresponds to the picture our ancestors had of an immaterial world of gods and is characterized by the unity of all opposites. The second Bardo consists of several stages, the two most important I will mention here. It usually starts on the 4th day after the onset of death and lasts until the 14th day. Just to be on the safe side, the Tibetans read all texts for all stages every day as the deceased passes through the individual intermediate states at different rates (according to their spiritual awareness) and time moves differently in those realms when compared to our material world. Consequently, even the deceased who awaken later to their new situation can still reach the first or second intermediate states.

"Dear (name of the person dying),
Listen to me and be here in all your attentiveness!
Although you may have died a few hours (days) ago,
I will continue calling you by name.
It will not bother you
If you have fully merged with pure CONSCIOUSNESS,
You will not need my advice.
But if the merest touch of individuality remains
My words will reach you.

Dear (name of the person dying),

Listen to me and be here in all your attentiveness!
Maybe you were not able to
Enter the emptiness of pure CONSCIOUSNESS
Because its brilliant light frightened you.
Maybe you shied away from the
Boundless serenity, power and love
Issuing from it.
Maybe you were not even able to perceive
The bright light of pure CONSCIOUSNESS,
Because you were dazed and confused
By the multitude of events and impressions.
Know now that you have left your material body behind.
Know that you have died.
Do not hold on to your old self
For love or weakness.
Take leave of your body and your old identity.
Let them go.
Let them go and know your true nature:
Pure CONSCIOUSNESS,
Without identity, without characteristics,
Without beginning in space and time,
Empty—and yet containing everything.
If you can rest in this knowledge,
You will attain eternal liberation just now.

Dear (name of the person dying),
You may not have been able to stay in that Oneness,
Or to hold on to the blessing of awakening
Despite the unity
With the clear light of pure CONSCIOUSNESS.
You may even have freely decided
To give up the blessedness of pure CONSCIOUSNESS
And to return to a world of forms and limitations,
To keep playing the cosmic game of evolution.
Whatever may have been your reason
To return to the path of manifestation:
Keep reminding yourself
Of the bright light of pure CONSCIOUSNESS.
Remember that your true nature
Is that pure CONSCIOUSNESS.
Remember that pure CONSCIOUSNESS
Is empty and has no characteristics,
While permeating and embracing everything.
Remember the force and the love emanating from it.
Remember that it is the origin
Of all optional appearances,
Born out of the pure joy of its own creativity.
Remember the oneness of all beings.
May these memories guide you
Through the experience
Of the denser intermediate states.
May they guide you through a future new life.

Dear (name of the person dying),

Listen to me and be here in all your attentiveness!
I will now tell you of the second intermediate state,
The "state of true being".
This is a very subtle state,
Emerging directly from the fire of vitality.
The "state of true being"
Is the original expression of pure CONSCIOUSNESS,
Its first manifestation.
And with it begins the separation of that,
Which truly is one:
The separation of that which is "observed"
And "the observer".
The "state of true being"
Is the perfect idea behind all forms,
The realm of divine archetypes,
The variety of cosmos before its unfolding,
The wealth of all possibilities.
This is where the six realms exist as seeds of potential,
As enfolded structures and impulses of development;
And even your being is a perfect potential,
Embracing all facets and possibilities.
In the "state of true being"
You will have visions and insights
That unveil the cosmic laws to you.
You will be able to understand the true nature of
All things, phenomena and processes.

You will experience coherencies
That you were unable to perceive
In your terrestrial life,
Because your body, your feelings, and your mind
Acted like veils that covered and limited your senses.
That veil has now been lifted by the death of the body
You have been liberated from these constraints.
Immediate understanding awards you with perfect knowledge.

You will recognize the "state of true being"
By its uninterrupted stream of layering vibrations.
They manifest as geometrical forms
Of brilliant light in all the colors of the rainbow,
By the forceful music of the true sounds of creation.
They conglomerate into shimmering balls,
Each with the potential to create
A perfect universe,
Reconciling all opposites,
Just to disappear again into emptiness.
They merge into one another,
Creating mythical patterns of perfect beauty,
And dissolve again.
Nothing is fixed, nothing is final, nothing is definite:
Everything flows and vibrates with love and joy.
You understand:
This is the creative unfolding of pure CONSCIOUSNESS
Which is found in the idea,

And that which you experienced in your terrestrial life
Was nothing but its faint shadows.

Dear (name of the person dying),
Pay heed and listen to what I have to say:
If you do not understand
That all these vibrations are but fleeting manifestations
Coming out of the emptiness of pure CONSCIOUSNESS
That you are yourself,
Then these lights will awe you.
The colors will scare you
And the sounds will frighten you.
You may experience its love and joy as pressure.
Its beauty may blind you so much
That you turn from it in panic,
Longing for limited perceptions
Of life on earth.
You may actually see hints of the material world
Shimmering through
—Not so glaringly, not so loudly, not quite so powerfully—
And yet it feels so familiar
That you long to return there.
Do not let it mislead you and do not confuse
The brilliant reality of true being
With its faint shadow.

Dear (name of the person dying),
Pay heed and listen to my words:
The key to finding serenity is this:
Relax,
Merge with the visions,
Without holding back or fighting them.
Merge with their flow,
And rejoice in their creative power,
But do not lose yourself in their contents,
And do not try to explain them,
But understand their true nature intuitively:
Everything that has a form or a name
Has been created by yourself,
A performance taking place WITHIN you.
They are your own creations,
Fleeting appearances
Coming out of the emptiness of pure CONSCIOUSNESS
That you yourself are.
Everything that you can perceive
Is you.
The perceiver and that which is perceived are one.
They were never separate.
Once you are able to understand
And keep this knowledge,
You too will find complete liberation right here
And merge with it for eternity in bliss and boundless love.

Dear (name of the person dying),
Understand now the interconnectedness
That rules the Kósmos,
Its perfect symmetry,
Reconciling all opposites.

Understand how the idea of separation,
The creator of dualities like light and dark,
Positive and negative,
Female and male,
Originates in the unity of pure CONSCIOUSNES.
Understand that each form creates its opposite,
To enfold it all again in the end.
Understand how the idea of space and time
Originates in the emptiness of pure CONSCIOUSNES,
A stage for the cosmic game.
Understand how the idea of the laws
Governing the game were born here,
As is the idea of the elements,
Serving as the virgin material for the actors and the scene,
And the idea of the senses
To perceive the game.
This is where the idea of emotions was born,
And the idea of the mind
To enjoy the game and learn from it.

This is also where the idea of the individual was created
As a part of the whole that cuts itself off,
Just to find its way back to unity:
From unaware to aware
To perfect self-awareness.
Look closely—who are you now?
You will understand that "you" do not exist
—Only a "true self": A potential,
Unformed and all-embracing,
No beginning, no end,
No past, no future,
No within, no without,
No "this is part of me and that is not"
—Only an awareness,
Embracing everything and aware of itself,
Here and now.

Dear (name of the person dying),
Pay heed if you want to remain here:
Do not give in to the temptation
Of wanting to control or direct the flow of visions.
Do not give in to the temptation
Of identifying with the limited content of an idea.
And do not give in to the temptation
To cut yourself off from the whole
And to become an active "I".
If you try to draw a line in space or time,
Or if you prefer one pole to the other,
You will fall out of Oneness
And you will experience the "state of true being"
In its imperfect aspect.
Remain in balance,
Remain in awareness.
Enjoy the blusterous stream of visions
And let them flow through you.
And if something terrible appears
Let it pass just as you let the blissful pass:
Without evaluation, without judgment,
In loving serenity.

Understand that this is the truth behind it all:
All that you can perceive in the second intermediate state
Are fleeting manifestations of the pure CONSCIOUSNESS
That you are.
Nothing lasts,
Nothing is of substance.
Visions come and go
— Like clouds, changed by the wind.
And your egoless self is the proto-substance
— The empty sky of pure CONSCIOUSNESS —
Background for the dancing clouds."

Dear (name of the person dying),
The moment you understand the true nature
of these appearances
You will awaken instantaneously.
If you can remain in this knowledge
It will liberate you for good.
You will realize the perfect state,
Beyond space and time."

It is possible that halfway through the second intermediate state, around the 9th day, the deceased can enter the next phase in which he will be confronted with the imperfect aspects of that state:

*"**Dear (name of the person dying),***
Listen to me and be here in all your attentiveness!
You may not yet have fully realized
the bright sphere of true Being.
The pull of the earthly world may have been too tempting.
You may not have been able to remain in loving serenity.
The wish may have been too strong
To become an active "I".
It can then happen
That you could experience the second intermediate state
In its imperfect aspect:
As the realm of the unredeemed shadows.
This sphere is the origin of all ideas
That man would call "bad",
But which are just incomplete:
Power changing into violence,
Clarity changing into cynicism,
Prudence changing into know-it-all
And passion changing into perversion.
This is where envy, greed and arrogance are born.
Hate and guilt has its origin here.
Here you are surrounded by dirt and disorder.
Here you will come face to face with the seeds of misery:
Ruthlessness and ignorance,
Blindness and stupidity.

You may come to the magical theatre,
The arena of mythical creatures,
Filled with beasts and demons,
Gods and devils,
Saints and witches,
Warriors and whores,
Wise men and children,
Who will leap at you, pressure you
And draw you into their dramas.

Dear (name of the person dying),
Do not fear these appearances.
Let them flow through you,
Without attachment and without refusal.
These creatures are also
Manifestations of your consciousness,
Incomplete parts,
Which, put together, will make up the whole:
Emptiness—without any features.
You are the master/mistress of this magical theatre,
The director of this fantastic comedy.
Understand its true nature:
Remember,
All appearances are truly empty,
Like your own being is empty.
And emptiness cannot hurt emptiness.

Dear (name of the person dying),
The knowledge of that which you called your self
Has been emptiness playing with itself,
Your identity was only a projection
Without endurance or substance,
This knowledge may deeply unsettle you.
You may be flung
Into a boundless space of deepest black,
Where you—taunted by sardonic laughter—
Will despair of your loneliness.
You may end up in a hall of mirrors,
Having to face a thousand facets of your own hideous face.
Instead of bliss you might be attacked by fear:
Could this entire Kósmos
Be nothing but the evil product of a weird mind,
Playing hide and seek with itself?

Dear (name of the person dying),
Know that you are still afraid of the truth.
Know that you are still clinging
To the remains of your old identity.
Try to understand the freedom arising from the knowledge
That there is nothing—no I, no You—
Nothing but pure CONSCIOUSNESS,
Unfolding in those appearances,
In the pure joy of its creative powers.

Know that your horrible fantasies are
But imperfect distortions of perfect ideas.
Know that you are still drawing boundaries,
Where there is all-embracing consciousness.
And know this to be the origin of all fears:
The separation between perceiver and the perceived.
But if you are all there is—what should you be afraid of?

Relax! Stop resisting!
Perceive all the horrible appearances,
As manifestations of all that,
Which you rejected or even cut off.
Transform them with your love, by understanding:
"That's also me—it's also part of me!"
Then you will be able to show yourself
In your complete form, in your entire strength and beauty.
And you will understand that they also, in their true nature,
Are empty—pure CONSCIOUSNESS.
Even if storm clouds darken the sky,
Behind the clouds the sky remains clear and unspoiled.
Dear (name of the person dying),
The very moment you understand this,
You will be awakened instantaneously.
If you can remain in this knowledge
It will liberate you forever.
Here you will also realize the perfect state
Beyond space and time."

The Third Intermediate State

Many dying people experience the actual withdrawal of consciousness from the body unconsciously, or in such an intense manner that—even though they may be aware of it—there is no behavioral form for it. This is followed by a phase of some confusion that may last several days. When the soul of the deceased comes out of that confusion, it has often not yet realized that its human life has ended. This happens most often when a life ends suddenly, i.e. in an accident, armed confrontations, etc., where there was no time to come to terms with death and dying. In such cases the soul may actually be in the subtle state but the pull back to the manifest world is still strong. This gross subtle area is also sometimes called "astral". Many of the perceptual as well as emotional and mental processes work much more smoothly since the material body no longer inhibits them as it did during their life on earth. The soul now has abilities that we know from lucid dreams, i.e. to jump in space and time, or to hear and see hyper acutely—independent of biological sensory organs. In fact, so much so that our biological perceptual organs—seen from that perspective—would more fairly be called "limitational organs". However, senses that are strongly related to the body such as scent and taste are gone. The soul enjoys its immaterialness with the advantages of being free from pain, the ability to move freely and to perceive the environment in an absolute manner—which often was impeded due to age and the dying process. But as the soul is not yet aware of having left its physical body, it often tries to continue taking part in the doings of the living. Its actions, however, no longer have any impact in the manifest world. This can lead to irritation and despair: Initially the soul is incapable of comprehending why it can perceive its material surroundings including all the people acting therein—but is not seen or heard by them. Sensitive people can perceive these fields of consciousness which were called "ghosts" in the past.

In this phase the most important task of the companion is to make the soul understand that its purpose is to take the path towards dissolution; in other words to help it to merge with the brilliant light of pure CONSCIOUSNESS. The other important task in the 3rd Bardo is to prepare the soul—irrespective whether it comes from the causal or the manifest state—for a possible new incarnation. That is why the third Bardo is also called the "state of becoming". It ideally begins on the 14th day after the moment of death and ends around the 49th day. That is not to say that the soul inevitably incarnates after 49 days, but rather that the soul by then is so safely on its way that the assistance can be completed. Stephen Levine has interviewed people in Asia who could remember their last incarnation and speaks of an average of 15 months until a rebirth.[1]

The following shows a few texts that describe the third intermediate state:

"Dear (name of the person dying),
Listen to me and be here in all your attentiveness!
Even though I know that you no longer exist
In the manner we used to know you,
I shall continue to call you by your name
So that my words may find you.
Maybe you have freely decided
To leave the state of pure CONSCIOUSNESS
To return again to a world of form and limitations.
Maybe you have also freely decided
To leave the state of pure CONSCIOUSNESS
To continue playing the game of life and evolution.
But maybe you left the material world
So unexpectedly and suddenly
That you have been confused and benumbed
And have just now regained your senses.
So listen carefully now: You are dead!
And though your mind may be free and acute as never before,
And your feelings brim over with intensity,
And your body feels healthy and agile
The way it no longer felt in life:
Look back—no tracks!
Look to the side—no shadow!
Look into the mirror—no reflection!
No scent and no taste!
Understand that you no longer have a physical body.
Understand that you are dead.

Dear (name of the person dying),
You may still be at the place
Where you died.
You may feel a pull to return there.
Do not, however, try
To intrude into the lives of your loved ones.
They cannot see you.
They cannot hear you.
Your actions have no effect whatsoever.
You have nothing left to do in the material world.
You have no more tasks and duties there.
What was left undone
Will be completed by others.
Understand that there is no way back
And let go of your old life.

Due to the capabilities you have in the third intermediate state
You are able to understand the true thoughts and feelings
Of those you left behind.
That may sadden or enrage you:
The grief of your loved ones may be so intense,
That you cannot bear it.
Maybe there is one who is gladdened by your death,
Or another with just an eye on the inheritance.
Your death may have caused strife and discord.
Maintain your serenity,
Beware of any complications,
Do not get involved:
This is no longer your concern!
Empathize with them and wish them the best.
Then turn back and be on your way.
Look ahead to the possibilities you will now have:
The knowledge of your self's true nature,
Absolute liberation
In the experience of pure CONSCIOUSNESS.

You may yet decide to stay in the "state of becoming"
And to prepare yourself directly for rebirth.
Whatever you may choose:
Do not look back on your old life
And your old identity,
But open up for the next step."

Dear (name of the person dying),

Listen to me and be here in all your attentiveness!
Wherever you may be right now:
I will now tell you about the third intermediate state,
The "state of becoming".
It is the sphere between
The formless "state of true being"
And the material world on earth.
It is the state
Where ambiguity becomes explicit,
Where ideas become terms,
Where laws solidify to become concrete forms.
These forms as yet have no substance.
Their bodies are composed of subtle energies.
And they are perfect in their being,
Which the limitation of the material world
would not allow for.
Know this third intermediate state by its light:
It is not the brilliant blaze
Of pure CONSCIOUSNESS,
And it is also not the colorful brilliance of true being.
You are instead surrounded by a dull brightness,
A soft light like a veil of mist.
Know this to be a sign
That you have entered into the "state of becoming".

Dear (name of the person dying),
The "state of becoming" is an astral state
Like the one you know from your dreams:
Space and time have no meaning
And everything is transparent.
The moment you think of something
You are already there.
Nothing can stop you.
Not only can you pass through mountains,
You can also see through them.
You are able to perceive things that are beyond your senses
And connect with them.
You are able to will yourself
To accomplish the extraordinary.
Your wishes turn into reality in an instant.
You communicate wordlessly with those like you.
You can read people's thoughts and emotions.
But do understand:
These abilities are not of your doing.
They come to you naturally.
Do not desire them.
Do not abuse them.
These abilities are a sign
That you are in the third intermediate state,
And they work no where but here.

Dear (name of the person dying),
You have a body again,
Without blemish and without fault,
But it is transparent
Like the world surrounding you.
You can hear and see like you never did before
And your thinking is astute and fast as the wind.
But if you have not gone through the cleansing process
Of the first two states,
You will hardly be able to use your abilities:
Your mind will be restless and volatile,
Defined by fears and desires,
Like a feather in the storm.
Your unguarded thoughts
Can create visions
That you wish you had never desired.
Your emotions will dither
Between ecstasy and pain
With unknown severity.
Your actions will be defined
By instincts and old habits.
You will want to cling to your old identity,
Your old memories, your old places,
And your old friends.
You may strongly yearn to return to
Your old life as you once knew it.
But this may cause you a lot of harm.

Concentrate your mind and let your feelings settle.
Let go of your old memories and habits.
They have no substance,
Just like all the other phenomena.
Let go of the old.
Open up for the new.
Open up to the unknown.

See your surroundings
—Know that they are part of you: A manifestation of your soul.
It may look mechanistic,
Dead and without any love to you.
You may think it dark and fearsome,
Or mysterious and challenging.
It is an expression of your former deeds.
Here, you will encounter whatever you have rejected before,
Because hate and pride controlled you.
Here, you will encounter everything
That you only perceived distortedly,
Because greed and conceit blurred your vision.
Here, you will encounter everything
That you didn't understand until now,
Be it through ignorance or lack of knowledge.
This is the other side of being,
That which is still needed for completion,
That which still wants to be accepted and embraced.

Dear (name of the person dying),

You may be watching your past life passing
Before your eyes just now.
Realize where you have been conscious,
And recognize, where you have allowed
The game to catch you.
You may envision a court of justice,
And your deeds are being weighed,
The good ones and the bad
—And the verdict is rendered against you:
"Guilty!", "Incapable!", "Stupid!",
And you hear derisive laughter,
You want to sink into the ground for shame.
You may try to tell a lie,
And yet at the same time you know
That it doesn't make any sense at all,
Because it is you who is the judge
—And how do you hide from yourself?

These nightmares are the remains of your selfish ego
That is not yet ready to relinquish control.
All judgments are nothing but projections
Of your blinded mind.
Nobody judges you but yourself,
But being too blind to see your true nature
And from your lack of love for yourself.
There is no guilt, there is no punishment,

68

Only the fleeting game of images
In the emptiness of pure CONSCIOUSNESS
—And YOU ARE this pure CONSCIOUSNESS.
The moment you understand this
You will be liberated.

Dear (name of the person dying),
You may be losing yourself
In the collective memory of Kósmos,
Into the space where all the memories of the universe
And mankind are stored—including yours.
You may burn out in the fires of the big bang,
Or in the collision of two galaxies.
You may die as a plant in the jaws of an animal,
Or as an animal in a slaughterhouse,
Or as a man on a battlefield.
If you still identify with your old ego
That evaluated everything to either be good or bad,
You will die yet a thousand deaths.
If you still identify with the
Vulnerability of a material body,
You will be forever afraid.
Remember that you have left
Your physical body behind
—So what could possibly happen to you?
Remember that you are pure CONSCIOUSNESS
—What could possibly hurt you?

Let the images flow through you,
Without attachment and without rejection.
Do not be afraid:
They are manifestations of yourself,
Fleeting games of pure CONSCIOUSNESS
That is your true nature.
Give up all your resistance,
Embrace the images in loving serenity,
And they will lose their horror.
Know their true nature: Emptiness.
Know your true nature: Emptiness.
Remember: Emptiness cannot hurt emptiness,
And all that can be named,
dissolves into the nameless.
The moment you understand this
You will be liberated.

Dear (name of the person dying),

Listen to me and be here in all your attentiveness!
If you want to find liberation now,
Follow this path:
Connect yourself to your true self.
Ask for understanding, strength and serenity.
Quiet your mind.
Ignore its chatter.
Do not follow its conditioned thought patterns.
Relax:
There is nothing to do.
There is nothing to think.
Understand the true nature of your thoughts:
Fleeting clouds in the sky.
Know the one who is aware of that:
Empty, pure CONSCIOUSNESS—primordial and brilliant,
Without beginning and without end.
If you cannot relax your mind,
Meditate upon an awakened master you love:
Buddha, Jesus, Mohammed, Ramana
—Whoever they may be—it does not matter.
Hear their words
That announce the one Truth:
"Form is emptiness and emptiness is form!"
"The Father and I are one!"
"There is nothing but Allah!"
"Truly all is Brahman!"

Understand that they do not identify with the drop
But with the ocean,
Not with the cloud,
But with the sky.
This is the highest truth.
Visualize your master,
Identify with him,
Merge with him.
Know that his liberated nature is yours
—Pure, empty CONSCIOUSNESS—
And the painful separation is but an illusion.
If you can internalize this understanding,
You will also find liberation right here.
You shall realize the absolute awakening
—Beyond space and time—
And you shall rest there in bliss and boundless love."

The Tibetans see the last phase of the passage as the definite preparation for a new life—when the final decision for another incarnation into an individual existence has been made. The following (and final) texts are devoted to this phase:

"Dear (name of the person dying),
Listen to me and be here in all your attentiveness!
You may have decided not to dwell in the
Timelessness of pure CONSCIOUSNESS
But to return to the material world.
You may wish to advance further,
To continue to play the cosmic game of evolution:
The unfolding of CONSCIOUSNESS in form,
From unconscious to conscious and
To the absolute consciousness of itself
As all that is.

Remember that there are six realms of existence
Where you can receive a new body.
The subtler ones are full of lightness and pleasure,
The coarser ones full of hardship and challenge.
Some may be more attractive to you than others,
They match your old conditioning.
But the familiar is just a repetition,
Not an evolution.
Some may repel you,
You may think of them as hard or foreign.
Select your new life deliberately and slowly.
Find the right balance of lightness and toil.
Do not let illusions mislead you.
The longer you delay your birth,
The better the choice will be.

The domain of man is located in the center.
It is the experimental field of the pure CONSCIOUSNESS,
The domain with the majority of opportunities for evolution,
And offers the most possibilities for realizing consciousness.
If you choose this domain
Focus on the blue sphere of man.
Be mindful of your visions of a coming life.
Choose an existence in wisdom and love.
Choose a life task that is challenging,
But that does not overtax you.
Do not follow the impulses of your old self
Which does not wish for change but security.
And let your true self guide you instead,
And focus your awareness on being
Born in a body and an environment
That will most serve your evolution
And that of Kósmos.
Visualize evolution facilitating circumstances,
Visualize parents who truly love each other.
Connect with your true nature—pure CONSCIOUSNESS—
And ask that the best
For the benefit of all may happen.
Know: If all form comes from pure CONSCIOUSNESS
And if you are pure CONSCIOUSNESS,
Then you have the power
To fashion your return back into matter.

Dear (name of the person dying),
Let go completely of your old self and
Open up completely to a new identity.
Do not let old thoughts, feelings and habits
Rule your new existence.
But preserve the old virtues, abilities and talents
That you have gathered
To help you in your new life.
Focus on that which you want to accomplish
—For your own development
And the benefit of all beings.
Dare to jump.

Do not be afraid
To choose the path of birth.
It is only the reversion of death:
You will briefly encounter the brilliant light
Of pure CONSCIOUSNESS,
Pass through total blackness
Into a cluster of cells.
You will exchange the freedom and liberty
Of your astral being for
The density of a physical body.
Try to do this in full consciousness:
The more you remain aware,
The less you will forget of your journey
Through the intermediate states,

The more you remain aware of your life's task,
The greater will be your chance to achieve absolute liberation
Even in the material world,
For the good of evolution
And all sentient beings.

This is all you need to know about the journey
Through the intermediate states.
Have a good passage.
And thank you for giving
Me the reason to remember:
Even though I still identify with an ego,
The essence of my being is pure CONSCIOUSNESS
And has never been separate from you."

These are the texts that describe the most important stations in the Bardos whereas my major concern was to show that both directions always remain open while passing through the different states: One towards the material world and the other towards pure CONSCIOUSNESS—densification and dissolution. The "Bardo Thodol"mentions both directions but only one is truly supported since the Buddhist—as mentioned above—would rather avoid a return to the material world. To me, both possibilities have the same value and the only reason that I give a little more attention to dissolution is that most people in our culture are not prepared for it. Furthermore, it is necessary to actively do something to achieve liberation whereas densification and rebirth basically happen automatically.

Our fast paced society will surely rarely give relatives the opportunity to read the entire text (printed in *italics*) over a 49 day period the way it is done with the "Bardo Thodol" in Tibet. In addition, as there is no linear time in the subtle and causal states, one may wonder if that is truly necessary. It is certainly most important in the hour of death. The urgency then decreases with each passing day. The Tibetans seem to view this similarly. I therefore believe that it is advisable to read the text once daily during the first 4 days. And yet you can sometimes feel by the atmospheric change in the room that the deceased has already "gone" after only one reading.

Usually the text is read to the dying or dead person at the place where he died. Even after the wake is over and the body has been removed, the soul can still be reached best at this location. One should call the soul by the name of the deceased to make it understand that it is the one being referred to. It also helps to visualize the deceased. This is easier if you place his or her picture in the room. But it is ultimately also possible to conduct an end of life ritual in the complete absence of the deceased. This is most advisable if the person died in intensive care or in an accident. In those cases it is best to mentally connect to the dying person—the soul is not bound by space and time. If you feel contact has been made, read the text to the deceased as though he or she is in the room with you.

On a final note let me say something about the further handling of the deceased's body: The Tibetans attach great importance to the care of the soul, whereas the body is given little attention. For the people there, the body has about the same significance as a car would for us: The driver (the soul) gets out of the car and selects a new one (new body)—the old car is scrapped without further ado. Therefore burials in Tibet are very basic and inexpensive. In the past the body was often simply laid out in natural surroundings for vultures and carnivores to feed on. Our western culture of death, however, has been shaped by Christianity up to this day. The concept of the "resurrection of the body" has caused our civilization to attach great importance to burials and to the preservation of the burial plot. This cultural trait, however, is changing. Many people now have their own idea of how they want to be buried. The new forms range from the anonymous tree burials to burials at sea. You should thoroughly acquaint yourself with this topic. There are undertakers who will meet the wishes of the deceased or those of the relatives.[9]

Addendum: Background Thoughts

Most people take our normal four-dimensional world as a given and objective fact. Unfortunately, all we know about our physical environment is what we can perceive with our restricted sensory organs and interpret with our brains. All objects and processes (i.e. colors, forms, sounds, etc.) are our subjective interpretations. They are, so to speak, the surface of something that obviously exists but the essence of which cannot really be recognized. And this means that we do not perceive reality but our subjective depiction thereof. We have also learned that it is the brain that produces our consciousness, that the latter is located in our heads, and that the body forms a border: Everything within that border is inside and everything else is outside. What follows now may seem a bit audacious: Couldn't that just be the crux of the matter? What if all our perceptions—including that of the body—are IN our consciousness? And what if there is only one single consciousness[10] INTO which we look, hear or feel through our multitude of bodies? And what if all objects, phenomena and processes we perceive therein only emerge from that subtle state of possibilities into a manifested consensus reality because of our collective(!) perception. What if they thus receive something like a "physical user interface"?(9) Shouldn't we then rather define the physical world of our perception as a state of mind of pure CONSCIOUSNESS?

Could it be that our manifested "individual consciousness" is not generated in the head, but that it is only a "portion"—or to be more specific - that information which the biologically limited brain filters out of the one single consciousness with the help of biologically limited sensory organs? What if pure CONSCIOUSNESS is simply the space of perception in which all objects and processes occur? Could it then be that there is no "inside" and no "outside" but only an unlimited continuum, and that only the human mind draws this borderline and that we then identify with one part of it calling it "I" while separating everything else from it as "Not-I"?[11] Why don't you try the following: When you open your eyes very, very slowly you cannot find a separation between what you perceive as your "inner" space of consciousness and your "exterior" environment (this experiment works even better for all other sensory perceptions). After all, we really do not see the objects of our environment "inside" or on the retina where they should be pictured according to the biological facts, but on the outside of the body. How does the brain do it? How does it get the objects from within the head to the "outside"? It could well be that these objects have never been "outside" but have always been within our space of consciousness, and that we have simply imagined this borderline between the inside and the outside. That would mean that we have thus created the illusion of being separate individuals facing an environment: In our self-evaluation, an infinite space of consciousness shrinks down to a tiny human "I". That is more or less comparable to an iceberg and only identifying with the "tip" and forgetting what lies below the surface of the ocean and the surrounding water because it cannot be seen.

Assuming that we truly are all parts of an infinite continuum of consciousness, why then is it so hard for us to understand that? That is probably primarily due to the understanding we have of Kósmos that has been formed in our society and finds its expression in language. These concepts act as cognitive filters that let us see only that which we want to see and are able to express verbally. For example, that includes that we—when we are awake—always have the feeling of being in the same body while our "surroundings" can easily change as we move our bodies around in our environment. However, someone who has to spend his/her life in one room due to illness might, however, might experience that quite differently.

But the main problem probably is our notion of how the brain and consciousness are interrelated. These days every child "knows" that the brain is just a computer that generates consciousness. What if that is not so, and the brain would simply be or work like a radio device that sends information and receives interpretations from the continuum of consciousness via sensory perceptions? So to speak into the "cloud"?[12] Chemically and biologically that would not change anything about the way the brain works and neurophysiologists would find the same results with their instruments. They would just be interpreted differently. And although that may sound a little far-fetched at first, this idea is not even that revolutionary: The same basics can be found already in Hinduism and Buddhism.

Examining our familiar concepts of the world in such a way naturally leads us to the question: Who or what is dying anyway? If everything that exists is pure CONSCIOUSNESS in its true nature, then dying could be an opportunity to transcend the cognitive identification with a restricted body-emotion-mind organism: The "physically" induced illusion of being an individual consciousness separated from pure CONSCIOUS-NESS would dissolve with death into a greater, supra-individual consciousness. That implies that we would always have to die first to be liberated from the illusion of separateness—not really a pleasant thought. However, there does seem to be a different way. But first we have to explore the question what individuality really is. Most people identify with their bodies, their feelings, the workings of their minds and their social roles. Bertrand Russell once suggested an extreme thought experiment, namely to strictly apply the scientific subject-object paradigm to oneself: I am the subject and everything I am able to perceive or observe are objects. Ergo, the material outer world consists of objects—evidently—and most of the time we also include the body in that assumption. But what about the interior world? What about my thoughts, emotions, mind patterns, social roles, my life story and my name—in short everything I "identify" with and call myself? I can certainly also observe these immaterial notions—so they are also just objects! In that case, what does that make me? Who am "I"? Who observes all this? This is the point in life where one could come to the conclusion that one's own innermost core is pure "egolessness" awareness—that which Wilber calls the "witness". Many meditation schools try to evoke just this insight with their exercises and it is usually experienced as an existential liberation.

It may well be that the most creative achievement of CONSCIOUSNESS is to have developed the brain-mind in man to the extent that it can simulate an "I" so convincingly that most people do not consciously perceive it—like a pair of glasses that you have gotten so used to that you identify with the glasses rather than with the person seeing through them.[13] The identification manifests in the form of experiences that do not simply happen—as for animals or little children—but are believed to be the individuals "own" experiences so that the individual thus believes that everything he or she has experienced is his or her very own experience. This trick—CONSCIOUSNESS with no memory of itself, stuck in the "individual" just to rediscover itself later on—is what makes the divine game so interesting. Wilber aptly describes that it is no fun playing chess against yourself because you will always know the next move of your opponent.[14] Splitting into different individuals would thus be an elegant solution. Following this logic, it would always be pure CONSCIOUSNESS itself that gains experience through the individual human being and that which is experienced is evidently also pure CONSCIOUSNESS because ultimately there is nothing but pure CONSCIOUSNESS: La ilaha il Allah! To "awaken" would then be nothing but the realization that the very own "I" is only a complex function of the soul, a definite object in the infinite awareness of pure CONSCIOUSNESS. And as the "I" must be very practical to be able to act in consensus reality, the solution cannot be to deny or destroy it (as some pre-rational religions would have us believe), but rather to transcend it. That means that we shift the identification from the limited ego to the indefinite CONSCIOUSNESS in which the ego—imperfect though it may be—is embedded as a practical little helper for the state of waking consciousness. Admittedly, at that point there won't be an "I" any more because whatever "I" perceived before to be "my" identity is then only a processes occurring in the indefinite, impersonal space of consciousness. If "I", however, in reality do not exist and the perceiving subject is pure CONSCIOUSNESS, and whatever is perceived (including emotional and mental processes) are nothing but evanescent objects and processes that occur and fade in pure CONSCIOUSNESS, then basically nothing can happen to "me"—not even when the person that bears my name dies. The moment "I" begin to identify with pure CONSCIOUSNESS—or in other words with the entirety of being, the entirety of all there is— that "I" will lose only an individual perspective of self-awareness when the human body dies—nothing else. The complete experience (e.g. as a near death experience) reconciles with the death, even when the individual ceases to exist. With this insight the game of life becomes really joyful.

Many people here in the West who believe in reincarnation have the notion that it is the identity that leaves the body when it dies and that it then reincarnates after a time. Therefore, you are still the same separate "person", who can even remember its former lives with the help of particular methods. The eastern concept by contrast says that the soul consists for the most part of karma and awareness and not of the identification with concrete, individual memories. CONSCIOUSNESS incarnates as living beings in order to develop and cumulate consciousness: from subconsciousness via selfconsciousness to superconsciousness. If then the soul is a form of CONSCIOUSNESS somewhere between the separate "I" and the all-embracing awareness per se, it must follow that its partial individuality is a finite aspect that can dissolve in CONSCIOUSNESS with the understanding of its true nature that is empty awareness. And that would mean that even the soul does not live indefinitely, but will find an end— even if that may be after many terrestrial lives.

Maybe this is our greatest fear in dying: To lose our individuality when we have worked our entire lives to become individuals. But then again, maybe it is the notion of a separate, autonomous individual that is the ultimate illusion of modern man. And yet we hold on to it with all our might for what would we be without it? To be only a small part in a cosmic game of becoming conscious called "evolution" from our perspective could be viewed by most people as yet another narcissistic wound. If the above assumptions are right, the complete death of body and mind could mean exactly this: to lose identity—the drop of water dissolves in the ocean—but not consciousness itself: CONSCIOUSNESS has become a little bit more conscious of itself by the life of one human being in the continuum of evolution.

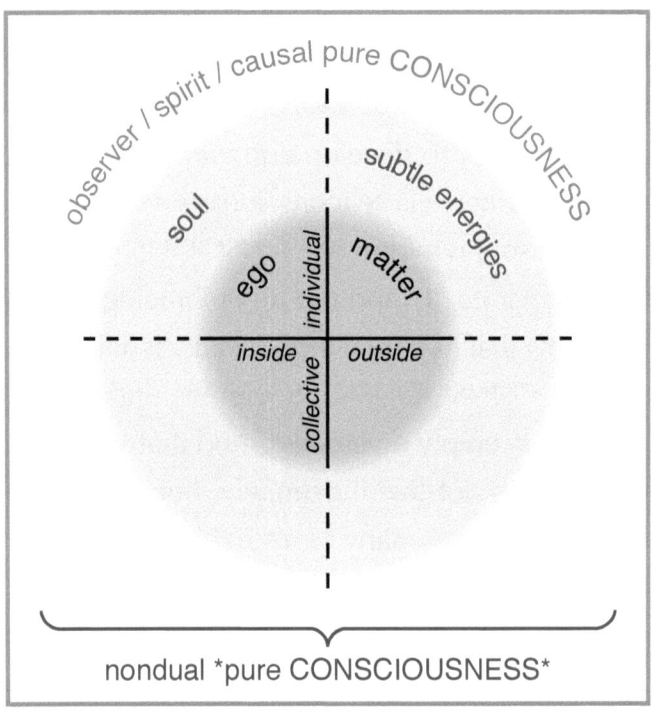

Adepts of Wilber's models might be surprised that the other structural elements (quadrants, levels, lines and types) are quite immaterial to this book. However, the emptiness of nondual CONSCIOUSNESS is absolute—beyond all structure, yet creating and containing all structure. The levels of consciousness would just determine how the human brain consciousness interprets its experience of the subtle to nondual states in the material world—yet this becomes obsolete with the death of that person. Even though evolution is probable in the subtle areas—and meant here is the development of the soul—it will likely follow different criteria than those followed by the manifest evolution of consciousness. I would further like to point out that the quadrants that give structure to our perception in the manifest waking consciousness turn transparent in the subtle state and are fully dissolved in causal or nondual CONSCIOUSNESS.

This is not only an elegant way to describe the increasing dissolution of the ego but also why the soul in the subtle state has access to the collective unconscious of mankind and other species as well as to the transpersonal patterns, ideas and hidden structures. You can gain access to the collective unconscious even as a living person through meditation, trance, dreams etc. so that memories of earlier lives do not necessarily have to be based on a personality that has been stable for several lifetimes. The insight the "Bardo Thodol" urges us to see that all manifest and subtle phenomena are ultimately nothing but fleeting forms of the causal pure CONSCIOUSNESS. This is what the integral school defines as "nondual": All that exists is in its true nature empty—even if it appears ever so material!

So, by now I may have confused you a little with my own conjectures. And, as it is impossible to verify unless you have experienced it all before (your own death included), I would like to stress the fact that these are conjectures even though there are quite a few indications that they are closer to the truth than our modern or rather "postmodern" notions of the universe. For a deeper understanding of dying, I believe it to be inevitable that we question the prevailing concepts and at least contemplate the possibility that everything we perceive may be just a huge information spectacle upon which our "individual psyche"—as an inseparable part of that spectacle—interprets matter, life and all the rest.

Ken Wilber: The Tibetan Book of the Dead

Wulf Mirko Weinreich's excellent interpretation of *The Tibetan Book of the Dead* is both well-done and very timely. It has been said that the single thing that human beings repress the most is not sex but death—the awareness of death. Many theorists, starting with Otto Rank and moving forward to Ernst Becker and then to my own work, have written extensively about the *immortality projects* that human beings create in order to pretend that they have avoided death and will live forever. Or, at the very least, pretend that they will not die tomorrow, and that pretense is repeated daily, thus giving the sense that they will never really have to face death, hence avoiding this most unacceptable reality forever.

In general, it seems that humans avoid the awareness of death in every moment by not living fully in that moment, but by pressing that moment forward just a little bit into the next moment, so their own immediate awareness always inches forward into a tomorrow-moment, or we could say, the present moment is stretched into a future moment. This actually amounts to a constant repression of death and a drawn-out living only in a temporal world.

Bear with me just a bit longer, and I'll tie this all up with *The Book of the Dead*. This constant repression of death works like this: Death, if anything, is the condition of having no future. It is the taking away of the future that triggers a massive death-sei-zure—that is, a panic in the face of being threatened by death, by having a person's future taken away forever. This is often referred to as a "cornered rat" reaction, because what you see in the massive panic of a cornered rat is exactly this fear of be-ing killed, this fear of death. And you can see this reaction in virtually all living things, fish to amphibians to reptiles to mam-mals to primates—to human beings. Even Freud came to this basic conclusion. Freud was working with emotionally dis-turbed clients, where psychic conflict was almost always pre-sent, and so Freud came to believe that this conflict was due to the fact that human beings have two fundamental but conflict-ing instincts, and it's the conflict between them that causes emotional problems. Freud at first thought that these two con-flicting instincts were food and sex (where food served the sur-vival of the individual and sex served the survival of the spe-cies). But those didn't quite work, so he changed them to ag-gression and sex (where aggression was life-denying and sex was life-affirming). But that didn't quite work either, so Freud finally settled on a formulation that he believed in for the rest of his life: the fundamentally conflicting instincts were *eros* and *thanatos*, life and death. Human life—all life, actually—was thought to be deeply caught in this fundamental battle between life and death, between living and dying. What you see in nature—exactly as with a cornered rat—is the incredibly strong drive to survival and a wild lashing out at anything and every-thing that threatens death, that threatens the end of survival itself.

Otto Rank was a member of Freud's original inner circle (a circle that seemed to be composed of nothing but flat-out geniuses. In addition to Freud and Rank, it included Carl Jung and Alfred Adler). Rank, in addition to introducing concepts like the "birth trauma" and "neurosis" (Rank actually invented that term), immediately saw the relevance of the battle of eros and thanatos, and created another phrase, "immortality project," to describe the actions that human beings took to avoid death, hopefully forever. In more recent times, theorists like Ernst Becker, in truly extraordinary books such as *The Denial of Death*, and Norman O. Brown, in his widely influential *Life Against Death*, pointed out with enormous clarity just how human awareness itself, in virtually every moment of its existence, is dedicated to this denial of death. I wrote a book called *The Atman Project*—the name itself was taken from "immortality project," but the concept was expanded just a little by pointing out how the denial of death was accompanied by a fight for life, with the ultimate life being "Atman," or one's fully awakened Self (I'll explain that in just a moment).

The point with all of those theorists is that, as I previously suggested, this death denial works in normal awareness on a moment-to-moment basis. One of the most universal conclusions reached by the world's great mystics and sages is that at the bottom of human awareness is an awareness of one's highest Self, which is said to be fully one with Spirit, and which can be directly realized by humans if they accept the death of their small, limited, separate-self sense (this "highest Self" is also the meaning of the word "Atman"). This realization or enlightenment is said to occur when humans can live above time in the "timeless Now" or "eternity." This timeless awareness or eternity is exactly an awareness that is free of death in the stream of time, because it is free of time itself. This "timeless Now" or "eternal awareness" is not some far-out and loopy mystical notion, but simply means being able to live in the present moment without obsessively focusing on the past or the future—it's the genuine Now moment or pure Present. This is such a straightforward notion that even the founder of logical positivism, Ludwig Wittgenstein, would put it like this: "If we take eternity to mean, not everlasting temporal duration but a moment without time, then eternal life belongs to those who live in the present."

Exactly. But look what happens moment to moment when we are caught in death denial. Death, we said, is the condition of having no future. So if we are trying to live in the present, but we are terrified of having no future, then resting fully in this present moment (or the timeless Now) is exactly what we cannot do—we must see a future in front of us, and so instead of resting fully in the Now, we push the moment forward just a few nanoseconds and experience it as an extended passing present—not a fully timeless Now but a timeless Now that has a little bit of a future, a pure Present that isn't just a present but includes some sort of thought or awareness of the next moment arising, so we can always push our present moments forward into some sort of future—thus avoiding forever a death-seizure. And this means that we are directly creating time, we are creating a temporal stream where we can always deny a timeless Now and always experience some sort of future unfolding before our inward eye. Time itself becomes our immortality project, a way that we can avoid being plunged into a timeless Now that has no past or future. This death-denial is a stunningly powerful drive, perhaps indeed the most powerful drive that humans have. Just hold your breath for a few minutes and see what happens. But the point is that, when we deny death Now by creating a future that always moves ahead of us, we inadvertently create a condition where we never can discover a truly timeless and eternal Now—hence a condition where we can never be enlightened.

In short, we are never awakened or enlightened or exposed to the realization of our highest Self and its supreme identity with Spirit. In demanding a future, in demanding a tomorrow, we effectively deny God now. We are condemned to an endless Great Search, with seeking—instead of awareness—our primary drive. We are forever condemned to live as our limited, broken, separate-self sense, projected through a temporal world that extends everlastingly forward in time, forever and forever and forever, never living Now or Now or Now.

Until, alas, it actually ends. After all, the skull of death will inevitably grin in at the banquet, and the picnic is ruined forever. This is exactly where *The Tibetan Book of the Dead* enters the picture. The core idea of *The Book* is that death is exactly what the mystics the world over have always said it was: the doorway to a genuine enlightenment, a real waking up, if we can only enter it with awareness. But when we are in cultures that are dedicated to the denial of death and lost in immortality projects, the chance of this authentic death-awareness diminishes drastically. It's true that, when theorists like Becker and Brown began writing in the 60s about the importance of becoming aware of death, we saw other researchers such as Elizabeth Kuebler-Ross introducing Westerners to the actual dying process itself, the stages that it usually goes through, and what people can do to both be more aware of this process and to help those who are going through it. Along with the theoretical books that I mentioned, these books had a significant impact. Among other things, a nascent hospice movement took root. There was also a rapidly growing interest in Near-Death Experiences, and how they seemed plugged directly into a genuinely spiritual dimension, exactly as the mystics had claimed. All of this was terrifically encouraging.

Cut to 60 or 70 years later, and it appears that Freud was right, and that this battle of life against death is so deeply rooted it could be thought of as instinctual. In our culture today, death awareness is again a rarely mentioned reality; its denial and repression is obvious everywhere; and immortality projects flourish wherever you look. It's not that human beings should have no awareness of time and just live in a nearly blind present moment. It's that human beings should be able to live authentically and fully in the present moment without always lamenting past moments and the guilt and sorrow that brings, or dragging in the future and all the fear and anxiety that brings. And the point about letting go of the small separate-self and finding one's own higher Self—and the sense of oneness with the entire world that the Self brings—is simply to be aware of one's own "supreme identity" and the profound joy and happiness that such awareness brings. And when it comes to the event of actually dying, the mystics are still right: as one of them put it, "If you die before you die, then when you die you won't die."

In other words, if you let go of the small self—which lives only in time—and discover your real Self—which is anchored in the timeless Now or eternity—then you have discovered that reality in yourself which is indeed timeless or eternal, prior to or beyond death itself. Thus, if you let go of that small self ("if you die before you die"), then it's very true that "when you die you won't die." That does not mean that there will be no physical death, it means that you will have discovered a higher Self that lives in the pure Present or timeless Now, prior to or beyond the stream of time itself. This is why this timeless Now is often said to be the "Unborn," because that which is born has a beginning in time, and the timeless Now has no beginning in time, it's "Unborn." And it is likewise everywhere said to be "Undying," because that which dies has an ending in time, and the timeless Now has no ending because it has no beginning, either, it's truly "Undying." This realization of an unborn, undying, timeless and eternal True Self that is anchored in the presence of a pure Present is the essentially common core of the world's Great Traditions—and it all comes down to how death itself is handled.

Dying to time, dying to the small self, dying to a limited and fragmented world—these are all the same death, according to the Great Traditions. This is completely obvious in *The Tibetan Book of the Dead*. What's so extraordinary about this text is that, more than any other, it understands that what happens after you physically die.... Well, here I need to interrupt and explain that, yes, *The Tibetan Book* does represent the Tibetan Buddhist tradition and how it understands reincarnation, physical death itself, and the stages that are said to occur during the overall dying process. In this sense, *The Tibetan Book* is dealing with things like the intense light that is a universal feature of Near-Death Experiences wherever they occur. But *The Tibetan Book* goes considerably beyond that, purporting to cover events that last, not just an hour or so like Near-Death Experiences, but up to 49 days after death and before rebirth. In this overall belief in death and rebirth, *The Tibetan Book* is simply reflecting an inherent Buddhist belief in reincarnation or transmigration—it is, after all, a Tibetan Buddhist text. In Tibetan, its title is *Bardo Thotrol*. "Bardo" simply means "in between," and "thotrol" means "death." There are all sorts of "bardos" in a human's life—there is, for example, the bardo or the space between two thoughts. But *The Tibetan Book* is concerned with the space between the death in one physical body and rebirth in the next one.

Clearly, stretching an account of what happens after physical death to cover a period of 49 days is largely hypothetical. After all, even Near-Death Experiences only last a few minutes to a few hours, maximum. But here's what is so astonishing about *The Tibetan Book*. The stages that are said to occur after physical death and before rebirth are the same basic stages that are said to occur in real life, moment to moment to moment, and these stages at least can be tested in this life by anyone who wishes to follow the recommended practice. The claim is that—and this part indeed can be tested by you or anybody who wishes to do so—each one of us starts out this present moment fully immersed in the timeless Now and the eternal Ground of Being that it discloses. But then, due to a primordial fear and grasping, we move away from this timeless Now and its Ground of Being and start to latch onto our small, limited, separate-self sense. According to *The Tibetan Book*—as well as many other sophisticated meditative and contemplative traditions—we move away from this timeless Ground through a series of steps or stages or levels, each increasingly less real or less authentic. We move from what Westerners would call "Spirit" (or the nondual timeless Ground itself) to "soul" (the beginning of a separate and illusory self) to "mind" (the elaboration and hardening of the separate self) to a material "body" (the end limit, the gross or physical realm, which is still a form of Spirit, as all of these stages are, but the densest, most removed and separated form). In the Eastern traditions, these stages are called "nondual," "causal," "subtle," and "gross." Thus, from Nondual to causal to subtle to gross, from Spirit to soul to mind to body— this is the path of our constant contracting and constricting, and the way out of this fallen world of sin and illusion is to reverse that path, by intersecting it at higher and higher levels, all the way back to Spirit itself. Otherwise, each of us starts this moment fully One with nondual Spirit, but ends this moments identified only with a separate ego and its physical body, and all the pain and enormous suffering that entails.

This "reversal" is essentially what meditation does. It is basically a pathway that trains awareness to be more attentive to larger and larger, or deeper and deeper, or higher and higher— take your pick—realms of interior reality, from the body to the mind to the soul and finally back to the pure Oneness of nondual Spirit itself. That is, meditative awareness moves from giving attention to all of the gross physical sensations in the body, to being aware of the mind or thought process itself in all of its forms and movements, and then into realms of awareness that are "beyond thought" (which are realms that basically explore the soul region, which is particularly marked by luminosity and endless love, illumination, and joy, even ecstasy)—and finally back to ultimate Reality itself, or pure nondual Spirit or divine Oneness. At this point, the entire sequence can then arise— Spirit to soul to mind to body, Nondual to causal to subtle to gross—but the person's awareness is no longer blanking out and forgetting the higher stages themselves. Rather, a person's awareness remains grounded in nondual Spirit, and is fully aware of the lower stages (from soul to mind to body) as they arise—but the individual is no longer lost in those lower stages or levels, but rather experiences them as what they are, wonderful and glorious expressions or manifestations of Spirit itself, to be enjoyed and be grateful for. All of the lower levels are no longer the source of grasping and illusion, detracting from their source as Spirit, but rather are seen as expressions of Spirit itself, as it throws itself outward to create the entire manifest universe, just for the sport and play of it all.

Now according to *The Tibetan Book of the Dead*, at the very moment of actual death, a person is fully thrown into a total immersion in Spirit itself, a complete Oneness with the clear light Void, and the entire sequence of manifestation then unfolds, exactly in the order that it normally does in real life. (*The Tibetan Book* often condenses Nondual and causal as one basic realm, so overall there are 3 major realms in the bardo sequence—nondual/causal to subtle to gross-reflecting, where awareness begins to see and adjust to the gross conditions and to the parents that will mark its coming birth in a physical body). The important point is that the moment of death becomes, not some sort of ultimate defeat, but a point where one can genuinely realize nondual Spirit, a point where one can authentically gain a real Enlightenment, Awakening, or Realization. It's said to even be easier to gain this Enlightenment in the bardo during the moments immediately after death. Why? Because it's much harder to deny death when you've actually just died! So a timeless Now stretches out endlessly before you in these moments. Your immortality projects are over; your death denial has temporarily been suspended; reality as it really is flashes throughout your awareness. Welcome to Reality! (It's this initial stage of the bardo realm that people are often seeing in Near-Death Experiences of a Clear-Light dimension—and this is exactly why seeing this spiritual reality in a NDE changes most people profoundly and forever, absolutely regardless of their spiritual beliefs before the experience—scientific materialists have NDEs just as often as spiritually oriented people do.)

The depth of this Realization will be made all the more likely and more profound the more that a person has practiced meditation or contemplation in their real life and thus has some familiarity with the higher stages of awareness itself. But everybody is plunged into this clear light Void in any event, and so this Realization is open to all. After the Clear Light flashes, then the rest of the stages of the bardo (the lower causal, the subtle, and the gross-reflecting) will then unfold, exactly as this would happen in real life. Further, if one has actually experienced an enlightenment or awakening during the immediate moments of death, then the trip through the rest of the bardo is done in full awareness, and among other things, this allows the individual to choose most of the factors in the bardo that will govern its coming rebirth.

This is not a totally insane idea. We actually have a very common example of exactly how this would work. The entire bardo realm (except for the Clear Light) is said to mostly unfold in a dimension that is a version of the subtle realm—that is, it's just like a dream state (which is also said to be an expression of the subtle realm). With a typical dream, most people experience that state in a relatively unaware fashion. That is, while they are dreaming, they have no idea that they are dreaming, and all of the dream's elements arise completely out of the control of the person having the dream. We might say that the dream does not occur in consciousness but is only the unconscious product of their past karma. For most people, who have not previously practiced some sort of meditative awareness, that is exactly how the bardo is experienced—it's just a dream over which they have no control at all, and so they are rather mindlessly reborn in a condition over which they had no say, and were driven instead by nothing but the sea of their own past karma.

But we know now that there is most definitely something called a "lucid dream." In lucid dreams, all of these factors change dramatically. For one, the person is fully aware that they are dreaming. It's a very conscious affair. For another, they can therefore choose the elements of the dream that they would like to see and experience. Want to fly? Just think that thought and you are immediately flying. Want to eat a fabulous buffet? Just give it a thought and the banquet is right there, all for you. Well, it's said to be very much like this in the bardo. If you recognize your own True Nature, the clear light Void, ultimate Consciousness itself, then the rest of the entire bardo will be in essence a lucid dream. You won't simply get hurled through it like in a typical unconscious dream, but rather you can meet it all with an aware consciousness, just like with a lucid dream, and thus you can choose a great deal of its elements, also just like a lucid dream.

I fully and strongly agree with Wulf Mirko Weinreich that not only great Tibetan teachers (or *tulkus*) can move through the bardo in this enlightened, conscious, and aware fashion, but that all people—as *The Tibetan Book* itself clearly says—who realize the Clear Light can do so. Thus all of us who are working on our own conscious evolution can look forward to the bardo as a realm where we can further that evolution, and if we are Awakened (either before death or at the moment of death) then we can move through the bardo in a conscious and aware fashion, guiding our own rebirth. And just as in real life, there are also great benefits to recognizing your True Nature at any of the lesser or lower stages (which appear later in the bardo). But the extraordinary thing here is that the overall bardo, just as with real life, starts out in its first moments fully one with nondual Spirit, and then moves "downward" into lesser realities, culminating in a dense, physically-oriented realm—and the higher in this sequence that you can recognize your own True Nature, then the more conscious you are, the more enlightened you are, and the better off you are in general. And *The Tibetan Book* shows you exactly how to do this, starting right here and right now.

This is why—for yet another extraordinary item about this book—*The Tibetan Book of the Dead* is not just a profound guide to dying, it is a profound guide to living. What *The Tibetan Book* offers us is a very precise guide to the mechanics of our own present-day enslavement, pain, and suffering. By going through this book, you will not only learn what the various realms look like that you might experience right after death, it will show you the very process—and its stages—that you go through right now, moment to moment to moment, if you miss or deny your own timeless Ground of Being, and thus end up settling for smaller and smaller, less and less free, versions of a separate-self (soul to mind to body). This truly is *The Tibetan Book of the Living*—if, that is, if you actually want an enlightened, awakened, joyful life.

Thus—and I'd like to emphasize this—even if you don't believe one single word of this *Book* in terms of anything that will happen to you in any sort of afterlife that you might have after you die, trust me when I say that you can believe all of it when it comes to the life you are living right now. It's an extraordinary guide to living an awakened life right here and now, moment to moment to timeless-Now moment. For this reason Wulf Mirko Weinreich has specially structured the book so that you can use it for your own daily meditations. The point is that the real bardo realm is not just occurring between this life and the next, it is fully occurring right now, between this moment and the very next. So if you can fully die in this moment, right here and now, you can be fully reborn and enlightened in the next. Each and every moment of this life is a Near-Death Experience, if we just don't continue to deny and repress it.

So I would summarize all of this by simply saying, welcome to one of the most extraordinary books ever written. And don't forget: If you die before you die, then when you die you won't die.

Literature and Links

1. Recommended literature on the care of the dying:
   › Looser, Gabriel: *Die Seele ins Licht begleiten*. (2001) München: Kösel
   › Levine, Stephen: *Who Dies?* (2. edition 1989) New York: Anchor Books
2. Used editions of *The Tibetan Book of the Dead*:
   › Dargyay, Eva & Geshe Lobsang: *Das Tibetische Buch der Toten*. (4. Aufl. 1984) Bern, München, Wien: Scherz
   › Fremantle, Francesca & Trungpa, Chögyam (Hrsg.): *The Tibetan Book of the Dead*. (2002) Boston & London: Shambhala
   › Hodge, Stephen & Brood, Martin: *Das illustrierte Tibetische Totenbuch*. (2000) Neuhausen am Rheinfall: Urania
   › Leary, Timothy; Metzner, Ralph & Alpert, Richard: *The Psychedelic Experience*. (2008) London: Penguin Classics
   › Rinpoche, Sogyal: *The Tibetan Book of Living and Dying*. (2002) San Francisco: Harper

   Also:
   › Varela, Francisco: *Sleeping, Dreaming, and Dying—An Exploration of Consciousness with the Dalai Lama*. (1997) Somerville, Massachusetts: Wisdom Publications
3. Recommended literature on the integral school of thought:
   › Wilber, Ken: *Integral Psychology*. (2000) Boston: Shambhala

> Wilber, Ken: *Integral Spirituality*. (2007) Boston & London: Integral Books
> Weinreich, Wulf Mirko: *Integrale Psychotherapie*. (2005) Leipzig: Araki

4. For the ease of readability this book has been written using male pronouns although both genders are meant. I ask for your understanding. The passages to be read aloud have been addressed to both sexes in some parts to make the adaptation of the text to the actual situation easier.

5. Parsons, Tony: *Invitation to Awaken*. (2004 Inner Directions Publishing)

6. Recommended Music

As music is of the utmost importance to me in this context, the following is a list of a few CDs that I personally deem perfect from beginning to end. Many artists should be noted for individual titles, i.e. Mathias Grassow, David Parsons, Akasha Project etc. And then there is certainly suitable music that I do not know. You will find audio samples for the CDs here listed on my website:

http://www.integrale-psychotherapie.de/musik.html

> Bob Downes: *The Inner Universe Vol. 1*

It´s a high point of music and my absolute favorite. The CD can only be purchased directly from the artist:

www.bobdownesmusic.de

A digital track can be purchased here:

https://bobdownesmusic.bandcamp.com

› Klaus Wiese: *Space, Clouds, Mercurius* and many others
https://klauswiese.bandcamp.com

› Aestrata (M. Grassow & T. Weiss): *Beyond The Veil*

› Mathias Grassow: *Dagaz, The Last Bright Light* and others
https://mathiasgrassow.bandcamp.com

› Stephan Micus: *Athos*

› Amelia Cuni and Al Gromer Khan: *Monsoon Point*

› B. Ashra: *Venus Meditation*

7. Strassman, Rick: *DMT—The Spirit Molecule*. (2001) Rochester, Vermont: Park Street Press

8. Since the word "soul" carries so many different meanings, it has not been used in the passages to be read aloud.

9. A few examples for alternative funeral homes in Germany:
› https://die-barke.de/
› https://www.horizonte-bestattungen.de

10. The quantum physicist Erwin Schrödinger termed it as follows in 1944: "Consciousnessis never experienced in the plural, only in the singular."

11. George Spencer Brown gives a possible mathematical description of the paradox of self-reference in *Laws of Form*.

12. Roger Penrose und Stuart Hameroff provide a spectacular explanation with the help of the Hameroff-Penrose-Model

13. Metzinger, Thomas (2009). *The Ego Tunnel*. New York: Basic Books. Deals with the ego as psychic construct.

14. Wilber, Ken: *One Taste*. (2000) Boston & London: Shambhala

Acknowledgement

I would like to offer my special thanks to Ullasa Irene Nelles and Tabea Plötz for their loving support. Very heartfelt thanks go to Ken Wilber for the essay and his many inspirations. I also want to thank Irina Hofmann, the editor of this book. Many thanks to the translators and lectors of the English version, especially Anke Bosse, Cindy Lorenz, Ilona and Michael Fuchs. My appreciation goes to all those people who helped me directly or indirectly to have and/or integrate experiences on the edges of the perceptible, first and foremost Osho, Gerd B. Ziegler, Lama Ole Nydahl, Stanislav Grof, Albert Hofmann and Don Ricardo Amaringo.

Dear Reader,

in our information saturated society, it has become very difficult to be heard without the backing of a powerful publishing company. Nowadays, many people get their bearings in the internet. If you believe that this book deserves it, I would very much appreciate it if you would take the time to leave your feedback with online-bookshops like Amazon or to write a short review for related websites or magazines.

Thank you!

Wulf Mirko Weinreich

Authors

Wulf Mirko Weinreich (born 1959) is a graduated psychologist and also studied religious studies, ethnology and sinology. In the 90s he lived in several spiritual centers for seven years.

In 2005 the book *Integral Psychotherapy* (Heiligenfeld Research Prize of the DKTP) was published, an attempt to bring together the different schools of psychotherapy based on the Integral Philosophy according to Ken Wilber. Since then, he has given lectures and seminars on integral topics. In 2009, *The Other Book of the Dead* was published, a religion-neutral translation of *The Tibetan Book of the Dead* into Western culture. He has also published articles in various scientific compendia and journals.

In his practice called "Praxis für Integrale Persönlichkeitsentwicklung" in Leipzig, he works mainly with interventions of Humanistic, Systemic and Transpersonal Psychotherapy as well as spiritual methods.

Information:

Email: kontakt@integrale-psychotherapie.de
Theory: http://www.integrale-psychotherapie.de
Praxis: https://www.psychotherapie-in-leipzig.de

Ken Wilber (born 1949) is the author of over twenty books and one of the most influential American philosophers of our time. He has developed a theory of the evolution of human consciousness. It answers the question why people perceive and interpret themselves and the world very differently. With his multidimensional model of consciousness, it is possible to depict insights of all peoples and times in one »theory of everything« without contradiction. He is the founder of the *Integral Institute*, a think tank for the study of integral theory and practice, as well as an inspirational figure and a visionary for the worldwide integral movement with its salons, institutes and initiatives such as *Integral Life* or *Integrales Forum*.

Publisher:
https://www.shambhala.com/religion-philosophy/ken-wilber

Initiatives:
https://integrallife.com
https://www.dailyevolver.com
https://www.integralesforum.org

Advertisement

Das Buch beschreibt ein umfassendes Therapiemodell auf der Grundlage von Ken Wilbers Integraler Philosophie. Die konsequente Verbindung von Klinischer Psychologie und Entwicklungspsychologie führt dazu, die klassischen psychischen Störungen als Stagnation der individuellen Entwicklung über die Bewusstseinsebenen zu betrachten. Die verschiedenen Störungen werden anhand des Wilberschen Bewusstseinsmodells neu klassifiziert. Der Assimilationsmodus jeder Ebene, der dem Piagetschen Modell der kognitiven Entwicklung entlehnt wurde, bestimmt, welche Therapiemethoden den größten Erfolg versprechen, was eine differentielle Indikation ermöglicht.

Die bekanntesten Methoden werden auf ihren Wirkungsbereich sowie ihren Interventionsmodus hin analysiert und zugeordnet. Ein weiterer Abschnitt beschäftigt sich mit den Grundlagen einer integralen Psychodiagnostik. Außerdem wird der Einfluß von Kontextfaktoren, wie Therapeutenvariablen oder die gesellschaftliche Einbindung, auf den therapeutischen Prozeß beschrieben. Die abschließende Analyse der Psychosomatischen Klinik Bad Herrenalb zeigt die praktische Anwendung dieses Therapiemodells als Evaluationswerkzeug.

Aufgrund der umfassenden Darstellung ist das Buch geeignet, integrativ/ eklektisch arbeitenden Therapeuten und Kliniken eine theoretische Begründung für die Wirksamkeit ihres Ansatzes zu geben. Weiterhin gibt es Ärzten, Psychologen, Psychotherapeuten sowie interessierten Laien Kriterien an die Hand, welche Methoden bei welchen psychischen Störungen am effektivsten wirken.

ISBN 3-936149-53-4 / 404 Seiten / 39 farbige Abbildungen / 2 Tabellen
2005 Araki-Verlag, Leipzig, € 24,80

111